Brain-Powered Lessons to Engage All Learners

Author

LaVonna Roth, M.S.Ed.

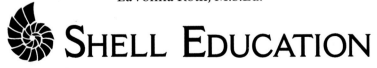

SHELL EDUCATION

Publishing Credits

Robin Erickson, *Production Director*; Lee Aucoin, *Creative Director*;
Timothy J. Bradley, *Illustration Manager*; Emily R. Smith, M.A.Ed., *Editorial Director*;
Jennifer Wilson, *Editor*; Evelyn Garcia, M.A.Ed., *Editor*; Amber Goff, *Editorial Assistant*;
Grace Alba Le, *Designer*; Corinne Burton, M.A.Ed., *Publisher*

Image Credits

All images Shutterstock

Standards

© 2004 Mid-continent Research for Education and Learning (McREL)
© 2007 Teachers of English to Speakers of Other Languages, Inc. (TESOL)
© 2007 Board of Regents of the University of Wisconsin System. World-Class Instructional Design and Assessment (WIDA)
© 2010 National Governors Association Center for Best Practices and Council of Chief State School Officers (CCSS)

Shell Education

5301 Oceanus Drive
Huntington Beach, CA 92649-1030
http://www.shelleducation.com
ISBN 978-1-4258-1182-2
© 2014 Shell Educational Publishing, Inc.

Table of Contents

Table of Contents (cont.)

A Letter to You

Dear Educator,

I want to take a moment to thank you for the inspiration that you are! As more mandates fall upon your shoulders and changes are made, I admire your drive, passion, and willingness to keep putting our students first. Every decision we make as educators should come down to one simple question: "Is this decision in the best interest of our students?" This reflects not our opinion, our philosophy, or our own agenda, but simply what is going to make the greatest impact on our students in preparing them for life and career.

As you continue to be the best you can be, I want you to take a few moments each day, look in the mirror, and smile. Come on—I know you can give me a bigger smile than that! Go for the big Cheshire Cat smile with all teeth showing. Why? Because you are sometimes your greatest cheerleader. Now, take that same smile and pass it on to colleagues, students, and parents. Attitude is catching—so let's share the one that puts smiles on others' faces! You will feel better and your day will be better.

Now, tear out this page. Tape it to a place where you will see it every. . . single. . . day. Yep! Tear it out. Tape it to the bathroom mirror, your dashboard, your desk—wherever you are sure to see it. Recite and do the following every single day—no joke:

I am appreciated!

I am amazing!

I am the difference!

From one educator to another, thank you for all you do!

–LaVonna Roth

P.S. Be sure to connect with me on social media! I would love to hear from you on these strategies and lessons.

About the Author

LaVonna Roth, M.S.Ed., is an international author, speaker, and consultant. She has had the privilege of working with teachers on three continents, sharing her passion for education and how the brain learns. Her desire to keep the passion of engaging instructional delivery is evident in her ideas, presentations, workshops, and books.

LaVonna has the unique ability to teach some of the more challenging concepts in education and make them simple and doable. Her goal is for teachers to be reenergized, to experience ideas that are practical and applicable, and have a great impact on student achievement because of the effect these strategies have on how the brain learns.

As a full-time teacher, LaVonna taught students at the elementary and secondary levels in all content areas, students in ELL and gifted programs, and those in the regular classroom. Her educational degrees include a bachelor's degree in special education—teaching the hearing impaired—and two master's degrees, one in the art of teaching and another in educational leadership. In addition to other professional organizations, LaVonna serves as a board member for Florida ASCD and is an affiliate member of the Society for Neuroscience.

As an author, she has written a powerful resource notebook, *Brain-Powered Lessons to Engage All Learners*, and is a dynamic and engaging presenter.

When LaVonna isn't traveling and speaking, she relaxes by spending time with her family in the Tampa, Florida area. She is dedicated to putting students first and supporting teachers to be the best they can be.

Acknowledgements

My family
My friends
All educators
Teacher Created Materials staff

I believe we accomplish great things when we surround ourselves with great people and take action. Thank you for all you do!

—LaVonna Roth

The Power of the Brain

"What actually changes in the brain are the strengths of the connections of neurons that are engaged together, moment by moment, in time."

—Dr. Michael Merzenich

The brain is a very powerful organ, one we do not completely understand or know everything about. Yet science reveals more and more to us each day.

As educators, we have a duty to understand how the brain learns so that we can best teach our students. If we do not have an understanding of some of the powerful tools that can help facilitate our teaching and allow us to better target the brain and learning, we lose a lot of time with our students that could be used to serve them better. Plus, the likelihood of doing as much reteaching will lessen.

This is where *Brain-Powered Lessons to Engage All Learners* comes in! The eight strategies included within the lessons are designed around how the brain learns as a foundation. In addition, they are meant to be used as a formative assessment, include higher-order thinking, increase the level of engagement in learning, and support differentiation. For detailed information on each strategy, see pages 12–19.

What Makes the Brain Learn Best

As you explore the strategies in this book, keep the following key ideas in mind.

The content being taught and learned must:

◎ be engaging

◎ be relevant

◎ make sense

◎ make meaning

◎ involve movement

◎ support memory retention

The Power of the Brain *(cont.)*

Be Engaging

In order for students to pay attention, we must engage the brain. This is the overarching theme to the rest of the elements. Too often, students are learning complacently. Just because students are staring at the teacher, with pencil in hand and taking notes, does not mean they are engaged. For example, we know that they are engaged when they answer questions or are interacting with the information independently with a teacher or another student. We don't always know when they are engaged just by looking at them. Sometimes, it's a simple question or observation of what they are doing that helps identify this. Body language can tell us a lot, but do not rely on this as the only point of

> "Even simple brain exercises such as presenting oneself with challenging intellectual environments, interacting in social situations, or getting involved in physical activities will boost the general growth of connections" (HOPES 2010, §2).

observation. Many teachers may have not gone into teaching to "entertain," but entertaining is one component of being engaging. As neuroscience research has revealed, it was noted as early as 1762 that the brain does change (neuroplasticity) based on experiences (Doidge 2007). It rewires itself based upon experiences and new situations, creating new neural pathways. "Even simple brain exercises such as presenting oneself with challenging intellectual environments, interacting in social situations, or getting involved in physical activities will boost the general growth of connections" (HOPES 2010, §2). This is fantastic if we are creating an environment and lessons that are positive and planned in a way that fires more neurons that increase accurate learning.

The Power of the Brain *(cont.)*

As a reflection for you, think about the following with respect to student engagement:

◎ What are the students doing during the lesson? Are they doing something with the information that shows they are into it? Are they asking questions? Are they answering?

◎ What is their body language showing? Are they slumped, or are they sitting in a more alert position? Are their eyes glazed and half-closed, or are they bright, alert, and paying attention to where their focus should be?

◎ Who is doing most of the talking and thinking? Move away from being the sage on the stage! Let the students be the stars. Share your knowledge with them in increments, but permit them to interact or explore.

◎ What could you turn over to students to have them create a way to remember the content or ask questions they have? What could be done to change up the lessons so they are interacting or standing? Yes, parts of lessons can be taught by having students stand for a minute or so. Before they sit, have them stretch or high-five a few classmates to break up the monotony.

Be Relevant

Why should the brain want to learn and remember something that has no relevance to us? If we want our students to learn information, it is important that we do what we can to make the information relevant. An easy way to achieve this is by bringing in some background knowledge that students have about the topic or making a personal connection. This does not need to take long.

As you will note, the lessons in this book start out with modeling. Modeling allows learners to have an understanding of the strategy and it also takes a moment to bring in what they know and, when possible, to make a personal connection. Consider asking students what they know about a topic and have them offer ideas. Or ask them to reflect on a piece of literature that you read or to ponder a question you have provided. For English language learners, this strategy is particularly effective when they can relate it to something of which they have a foundational concept and can make a connection to what they are learning. The language will come.

Make Sense

Is what you are teaching something that makes sense to students? Do they see the bigger picture or context? If students are making sense of what they are learning, a greater chance of it moving from working memory to long-term memory will increase. Some students can be asked if the idea makes sense and if they clearly understand. If they are able to explain it in their own words, they probably have a good grasp on metacognition and where they are in their learning. Other students may need to be coached to retell you what they just learned.

The Power of the Brain *(cont.)*

Make Meaning

Once students have had an opportunity to make sense of what they are learning, provide an opportunity for them to make meaning. This means that they have a chance to apply what was learned and actually "play" with the skills or concepts. Are they able to complete some tasks or provide questions on their own? Are they ready to take the information to higher levels that demonstrate the depth of understanding? (Refer to Webb's Depth of Knowledge for some additional insight into various levels of making meaning on pages 22–23.) For some students, simply asking a few questions related to what is being taught or having them write a reflection of what was just explained will allow you to check in on their understanding to see where they are before taking their thinking to a higher or a deeper level.

Involve Movement

This one is particularly important because of the plethora of research on movement. Dr. John Ratey wrote the book *Spark*, which documents how student achievement soars based on some changes made to students' physical education program in which students achieved their target heart-rate zone during their physical education time. Movement, particularly exercise, increases brain-derived neurotrophic factors (BDNF) that increase learning and memory (Vaynman, Ying, and Gomez-Pinilla 2004).

Knowing that getting students to achieve their target heart rate zone is not always an option, do what you can. Have students take some brain breaks that heighten their heart rate—even if for just a minute.

Movement has strong retention implications in other ways. Students can create a gesture connected to the lesson concept, or they can stand and move while they make meaning from what they learned. Movement is multisensory, thus, various regions of the brain are activated. When multiple brain pathways are stimulated, they are more likely to enter long-term potentiation from activating episodic and semantic memories.

If you come across a model lesson in this book in which not much movement is shared, or you find your students have been sitting longer than you may wish (you will know because their body language will tell you—unfortunately, we should have had them moving before this point), my challenge to you is to think of what movement you can add to the lesson. It could involve a gesture, a manipulative, or physically getting up and moving. If you are concerned about them calming back down, set your expectations and stick to them. Keep in mind that often when students "go crazy" when permitted to move, it's probably because they *finally* get to move. Try simple techniques to bring students back into focus. "Part of the process of assisting children in developing necessary skills is getting to the root of why they behave as they do" (Harris and Goldberg 2012, xiv).

The Power of the Brain *(cont.)*

Support Memory Retention

If we want our students to retain what we teach them, then it is important that we keep in mind what causes our brains to retain that information.

Key Elements to Memory Retention	Why
Emotions	We can create an episodic memory when we connect emotions to our learning.
Repetition	Repetition increases memory as long as there is engagement involved. Worksheets and drill and kill do not serve long-term memory well.
Patterns/Organization	When our brains take in messages, they begin to file the information by organizing it into categories.
Personal connection	Linking learning to one's self is a powerful brain tool for memory. This, too, can be tied to emotion, making an even stronger connection.
Linking new and prior knowledge	Taking in new information automatically results in connecting past knowledge to what is new.

(Roth 2012)

As you explore the strategies and lessons throughout this book, note how many of them incorporate the keys to memory retention and what engages our students' brains. As you begin to explore the use of these strategies on your own, be sure to keep the framework of those important components.

The bottom line—explore, have fun, and ask your students how they feel about lessons taught. They will tell you if they found the lesson interesting, engaging, and relevant. So get in there, dig in, and have some fun with your students while trying out these strategies and lessons!

It's All About Me
Strategy Overview

Think about the last argument you had with someone. Now, think about your happiest moment. Did the feelings come rushing back and your heart rate speed up, or did an expression cross your face? That is the power of emotion. Science has discovered "that the two structures of the brain that are mainly responsible for long-term memory are located in the emotional area of the brain" (Sousa 2006). Therefore, we need to do what we can to tie content to emotions so that the brain has a greater chance of storing what we teach for the long term.

In addition to emotion, movement and repetition are key to memory retention. In the *It's All About Me* strategy, students take a content area, recall what they already know (or predict what the content entails), and then find ways to make it personal. By making the connection personal, they tie it to a memory they have about someone or something. Be careful that students do not tie it to something personal that was stressful for them, as this can actually hinder the learning. Remember, learning occurs when a positive emotional response is experienced and dopamine, a feel-good chemical, is released. Neuroscience teaches us to incorporate emotions with our cognitive learning because it leads to "the most efficient and effective learning" (Immordino-Yang and Faeth 2010, 74).

Strategy Insight

This strategy takes students through a process that exposes the content to be learned through multiple modalities: visual, auditory, kinesthetic, emotional, and, in some lessons, tactile. The way each lesson is modeled varies depending upon age group, but the core strategy remains consistent throughout all of the lessons. When a movement is learned and we tie it to something personal, we increase the chance of retaining the learning. Movement takes learning from abstract to concrete. It is about students and their connection to the world. Students may copy others, and that is acceptable as long as they can explain the connections and relate it to themselves, personally. Learning to make a personal connection to something is not always easy and usually takes practice.

Teacher Notes

◎ It is important to work with students on difference of opinion here and to respect another person's thoughts and opinions. Students may not understand another student's personal connection, and that is acceptable. You may want to role-play how to respect someone else by teaching them to say something such as "I had not thought of it that way," or "I am glad you found a way to help you understand what we are studying," or "Thank you for sharing with me."

◎ Since this is a personal connection, respect students' privacy. They may create a way to remember that they do not want to share with you. Encourage them to brainstorm a way that can be shared.

ABC Professors
Strategy Overview

This strategy is best used after students have studied a topic. They become "professors" or "experts" because they have the knowledge base that is necessary to complete a task about the topic.

After students are taught what they need to know, have them begin thinking about the topic. Portions of the strategy are modeled. Then students, with guidance, brainstorm words or phrases about their topic that begin with each letter of the alphabet. The goal is to have a word or phrase for each letter of the alphabet filled in on their *ABC Professor Notes* activity sheet (page 62). This strategy is motivating and can ease the challenging task of asking more inquisitive questions.

Strategy Insight

Although this strategy is meant as a review, it could be used as a formative preassessment to see what students know before a topic is introduced and then used again to see the growth that occurred after teaching the topic. Once students are comfortable with the strategy, they can be given the opportunity to choose their own topic (McCombs 1997).

This strategy can be used as a "sneak peek" to find out what students know, but teachers should watch for the level of frustration. When too much frustration occurs, the stress blockers begin to hinder thinking, and learning declines (Medina 2008). Teachers should challenge students so that their brains seek the pleasure of the intrinsic rewards of learning. According to Csikszentmihalyi (1996), teachers need to keep students in the "flow," a level of challenge that is not too high or low and one that keeps them motivated and engaged, as well.

During the Evaluate/Create component of the strategy, students are challenged to ask questions in alphabetical order and provide a response to the questions their partners ask. Students do not necessarily need to answer the questions. This strategy is to get them thinking and wondering, becoming curious enough to seek answers or speculate about possible answers.

Teacher Notes

◎ Not every box needs to be filled when completing the *ABC Professor Notes* activity sheet. Instead of limiting the number of letters or excluding certain letters, make it a challenge for certain identified students to see how many quality words or phrases they can think of. If it becomes apparent that they have reached a high level of frustration, then ask them which boxes they would like to reasonably eliminate.

◎ If using this as a priming activity, have students record their responses so that they can assess what they used to think, what they now think, and the depth of learning that occurred as they reflect back.

It Takes Two
Strategy Overview

In this strategy, students compare and contrast two topics (e.g., stories, historical figures, types of clouds and shapes) using a T-chart and sticky notes. The goal is for students to analyze each topic and create a chart that represents their thinking. Thereafter, another group of students will evaluate whether it agrees with the original group's thoughts or, if not, if it is going to propose another way to think about the topic. The goal is for students to be able to think at a higher level by justifying either what each sticky note says and where each one is placed or if it qualifies to be on the T-chart at all.

Strategy Insight

Organization and thinking critically are key components in this strategy. Since we organize ideas in our brains systematically and create a neural pathway as more modalities are used, students increase their learning by seeing the information, sorting through what is important, organizing the facts by what is similar and what is different, and adding another level of value through student interaction (Van Tassell 2004). Each of these components plays an integral part in student engagement and retention (Covington 2000). It is another way for students to work with content at a level that is minds-on and hands-on.

Using sticky notes during this activity is important (as opposed to recording the similarities and differences on a sheet) because students' thinking will shift as they discuss and learn more. The sticky notes allow the graphic organizer to become manipulative, and it is a new way for them to see if they agree or disagree with their classmates and adjust accordingly.

Teacher Notes

◎ It is imperative that teachers observe during all stages of the lesson. This provides the feedback we need to determine the next direction of instruction. In addition, it allows an opportunity to guide students in their thinking, as some may struggle with concepts at a higher level. **Note:** Do not guide too much. A large part of learning is struggling through the process with a small amount of frustration but not so much that students give up.

◎ During discussions, students will likely discover that there can be more than one answer. That is where collaboration and cooperation pay off.

◎ For younger students, reconvene as a whole group and model the evaluation steps, using one group's chart.

Matchmaker
Strategy Overview

The importance of movement and having students get up out of their seats cannot be emphasized enough. Thus, here is another strategy that allows our students to do so. *Matchmaker* also provides students an opportunity to get repeated practice in an environment in which the repetition is guided and correct. This means that when students practice repeatedly, the likelihood of recall increases. A key factor here is that it must be correct practice. When students do this activity with one another, they are getting a chance to see repeated practice with automatic feedback provided about whether they are correct or not.

Strategy Insight

Every student is given an address label to wear. Each label is a vocabulary word, a concept, a formula, etc. On index cards are the matching definitions, illustrations, examples, synonyms, etc.

Students wear the address labels and stand in a circle with the index cards on the floor in the middle. Students hold hands and bend down to pick up an index card with their connected hands. Without letting go, they have to get the card they picked up to the correct person, according to his or her address label. This strategy can be repeated as many times as you wish to help students practice.

Teacher Notes

◎ An alternative to this is for students to not hold hands when they pick up a card. However, energy and engagement increase with the added challenge of holding hands and not letting go.

◎ Be sure to listen in and encourage students to discuss disagreements or to have them respond to a reason why a particular card goes with another card.

Just Say It
Strategy Overview

Working together and hearing thoughts and language are beneficial to all learners, but these things can be especially beneficial to English language learners. *Just Say It* permits students not only to use what they have read, written, or heard but to have a chance to use listening skills for the content as well. A challenge layer to this strategy is having students hold back on a response for a period of time. This allows the one student to say what he or she needs to say before the partner inflicts his or her opinion or factual information upon him or her. It teaches the skill of patience, listening, and being open to others' thoughts at the same time.

Strategy Insight

Students are to respond to their partners, providing feedback and information on a given topic (e.g., a writing prompt, thoughts, an idea). Have students sit facing their partners (sitting at desks is preferable). Identify Partner *A* as the person closest to the front of the room and Partner *B* as the person closest to the back of room. Have Partner *A* start. Partner *A* shares his or her thinking with Partner *B* as Partner *B* only listens for 30 seconds. After 30 seconds, Partner *B* responds to Partner *A*. They then switch roles—Partner *B* shares while *A* listens. Then *A* provides insight or feedback. Students should record (during or at the end) what their partners say for further consideration and use that to write about the topic.

Teacher Notes

◎ You may wish to shorten or lengthen the time each partner has, depending upon the topic and age.

◎ Using a timer, a train whistle, or a bell is a great way to help partners know when to switch, since conversations may get lively or partners may tune out other nearby sounds.

Reverse, Reverse!
Strategy Overview

Reverse, Reverse! is meant to be a challenging strategy. When students are under stress, there will often be not only a chemical but a physical change in the brain. Students must learn the skills to deal with stress, but in a safe and friendly environment. In this strategy, students will practice the speed and fluency of facts, but they will do so under pressure—a pressure that you can adjust or increase, depending upon the topic and age level of your students.

Strategy Insight

Students sit or stand in a circle. They are given a topic and asked to brainstorm what they know about it. One student begins by sharing a fact about the topic. Going clockwise, the next student must quickly say another fact related to the one just stated. If the student pauses more than five seconds or states an incorrect fact, the student who just finished must state the next fact (reversing the direction of participation). One student sits out to judge the facts and make sure rules are followed. Continue until participation stalls. For example, a math activity using this strategy can include counting by threes. The first student says, "3;" the next student says, "6;" the next says, "9." If the following student says, "13," the rotation reverses to the previous student, who must say, "Reverse," and must also say the correct answer, "12." The responses are now going counterclockwise. An example of using this strategy in social studies can include the three branches of government. The first student might say, "Legislative branch;" the second says, "Makes the laws;" the third student says, "Congress;" and the fourth says, "Checks and balances." The judge (student sitting out) can halt the flow to ask how the response relates to a previously said fact. If justified, the round continues. *Reverse, Reverse!* continues until a predetermined amount of clock time or number of times around the circle has been met.

Teacher Notes

◎ It is important to set the stage for students to feel safe when using this strategy. You may wish to take out the reverse portion at first and work on just the speed. Add the extra layer of difficulty for novelty and time-pressured practice.

◎ For younger students, you may choose to not have the next student say, "Reverse," but instead state the correct fact.

WPH Accordion
Strategy Overview

Think of a mystery story. Who or what is involved? What do you predict will happen? What does happen? These questions make up the *WPH Accordion* strategy. Each of these components plays a key part in motivation, engagement, and memory.

Asking *who* or *what* is involved (*W*) prepares our brains to think about the topic. Who or what could be involved in the story, event, experiment, or solution? This question piques our brain's interest because we want to know. The brain likes to learn (Willis 2008).

What do you *predict* (*P*) will happen? Our brains love to predict and to get it right. When our predictions are right, dopamine receptors are activated and our brain experiences that as pleasurable, which increases our reward response (Rock 2009). Emotions come into play, which is important for long-term memory (Jensen 2005). When our predictions are wrong, dopamine levels reduce and the brain works to remember it correctly so it can have the pleasure from dopamine rising (Willis 2008).

What actually *happens (H)*? The brain receives the message whether the prediction is right or not. Our brains use this information for future predictions. Did what we think was going to happen occur?

Strategy Insight

When working with students, it is important to create a culture in which it is okay to be wrong. Often, predictions are wrong; it is how we react that makes a difference. What matters is what we do with that information. If students pull what they know from background knowledge to figure out a mystery component and if they ask questions based on what they know, then that is a start to making good predictions. Teachers should empower students to become aware of what they know and what they are thinking, and that being wrong tells their brains to pay attention to the correct way (Flavell 1979; Willis 2008; Baker 2009).

Students work with topics that have a twist or an unexpected outcome. This allows us to think logically about a solution and also pulls information from the creative side of our brains. Teachers need to encourage students to do their own thinking, ask questions, and work to figure out the result.

Teacher Notes

◎ Provide students the option to draw or write in order to meet the differentiation needs of learners.

◎ You may need more than two sets of the WPH Accordion. If more than two sets are needed, accordion-fold the other half-sheet of paper and tape it to the end of the first accordion. This gives you four sets of W-P-H sections.

That's a Wrap!
Strategy Overview

It is important to teach students how to study. Studying can be boring, primarily because it involves repetition. But repetition is one of the keys to memory, as it makes the connections in our brains stronger (Jensen 2005). Willis (2008) further developed this idea by stating that when a greater number of neural connections are activated by the stimulation of practice, an increased number of dendrites grow to strengthen the connections between the neurons.

Strategy Insight

That's a Wrap! is a strategy that helps students learn how to study and how to mix up the repetition with a little fun. Students pull important information, put it into the form of a question, and then write an interview in the form of a script. The interview can be performed in front of the class or other classes, or students can practice at home, using different voices.

Be sure to model. It takes guidance and practice to whittle down information to the key facts or questions. Walk students through the steps to define what is important instead of what is simply a fun fact. Do the facts directly help to answer the essential questions?

As this strategy progresses, encourage students to think about and write questions that are more open-ended than closed-ended. Ainsworth (2003) states that *open-ended* means more than one answer or solution. *Closed-ended* is one answer or solution, often a yes/no response. Open-ended takes more time and more thinking because several factors are taken into consideration; it is not just one simple answer.

If the teacher wants to know if students have moved the learning from working memory to long-term memory, quiz them after 24 hours. If students can recall the information or idea with no advance notification, then the content is making its way into long-term storage. On the same note, this "pop quiz" can be used to check what they remember, and it should not be graded. It is a formative assessment for students to determine what they still need to study.

Teacher Notes

◎ Remember, emotions are a key to increasing memory, along with repetition. As students write the script and rework it, they are repeatedly seeing the information.

◎ Model the cue often used by teachers: Pause when something key is about to be presented. State, "This is important" or "This will be on the test." If information is written on the board, change colors when writing the important fact.

How to Use This Book

Lesson Overview

The following lesson components are in each lesson and establish the flow and success of the lessons.

Icons state the brain-powered strategy and one of the four content areas addressed in the book: language arts, mathematics, science, or social studies.

Each lesson revolves around one of the eight **brain-powered strategies** in this book. Be sure to review the description of each strategy found on pages 12–19.

Vocabulary that will be addressed in the lesson is called out in case extra support is needed.

The **procedures** provide step-by-step instructions on how to implement the lessons successfully.

The **standard** indicates the objective for the lesson.

A **materials** list identifies the components of the lesson.

Many lessons contain a **preparation note** that indicates action needed prior to implementing the lessons. Be sure to review these notes to ensure a successful delivery of the lesson.

The **model** section of the lesson provides teachers the opportunity to model what is expected of students and what needs to be accomplished throughout the lesson.

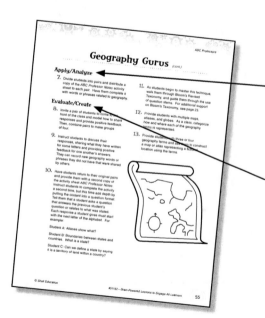

The **apply/analyze** section of the lesson provides students with the opportunity to apply what they are learning as they analyze the content and work toward creating a personal connection.

The **evaluate/create** section of the lesson provides students with the opportunity to think critically about the work of others and then to take ownership of their learning by designing the content in a way that makes sense to them.

How to Use This Book *(cont.)*

Lesson Overview *(cont.)*

Some lessons require **activity cards** to be used. You may wish to laminate the activity cards for added durability. Be sure to read the preparation note in each lesson to prepare the activity cards, when applicable.

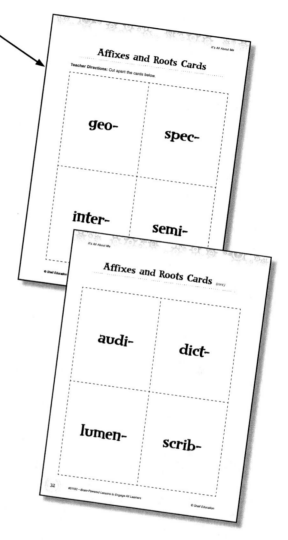

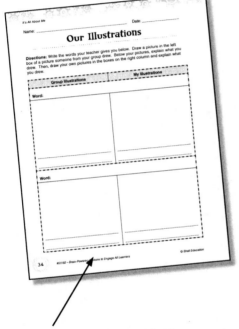

Activity sheets are included for lessons that require them. They are to be used either in groups, individually, or just by the teacher. If students are working in groups, encourage them to create a group name to label the activity sheet.

All of the activity sheets and additional teacher resources can be found on the **Digital Resource CD**.

How to Use This Book *(cont.)*

Implementing Higher-Order Thinking in the Lessons

What Is Higher-Order Thinking?

Higher-order thinking occurs on a different level than memorizing facts or telling something back to someone exactly the way it was told (Thomas and Thorne 2009). As educators, it is important to be aware of the level of thinking that students are asked to do. If teachers record the number of questions they ask students on a recall or restate level as well as how many were asked at a higher level, they may be surprised at the imbalance. How do they expect students to think at a higher level if they are not challenged with higher-order questions and problems? Students should be given questions and assignments that require higher-order thinking.

Higher-order thinking also involves critical thinking. If teachers want students to remember facts and think critically, they need to have them be engaged and working with the content at a higher level so that it creates understanding and depth. In addition, higher-order thinking and critical thinking are imperative to 21st century skills. Employers want workers who can problem-solve and work cooperatively to find multiple solutions. The lessons in this resource gradually place more ownership of the learning process in the hands of students as they simultaneously move through higher-order thinking.

Bloom's Taxonomy and Webb's Depth of Knowledge

Throughout the history of education, structures were created to guide teachers in ways to evoke higher-order thinking. Two of the more popular structures are Bloom's Taxonomy and Webb's Depth of Knowledge (DOK).

Benjamin Bloom developed Bloom's Taxonomy as a way to classify educational learning objectives in a hierarchy. In 2001, Lorin Anderson, a former student of Bloom's, worked with some teachers to revise Bloom's original taxonomy by changing the terminology into verbs and switching the top two levels so that *create* (synthesis) is at the top and *evaluate* (evaluation) is just below (Overbaugh and Schultz n.d.).

Norman Webb created Depth of Knowledge in 1997 in order to assist with aligning the depth and complexity of a standard with its assessment. This structure focuses on how the verb is used in the context of what is asked of the student (Webb 2005). DOK correlates with Backwards Planning (Wiggins and McTighe 2005) in that the standards are addressed first and then an assessment that targets the standards is developed or selected.

How to Use This Book *(cont.)*

It is important that teachers instruct students at cognitive levels that meet their needs while challenging them, as well. Whether students are below level, on level, or above level, teachers should use the tools necessary to help them succeed. Using Webb's DOK gives us the tools to look at the end result and tie complexity to the assessment. Bloom's Taxonomy helps to guide depth of assignments and questions. Where the two meet is with the word complexity. Complexity is rigor. Complexity is the changing of levels within Bloom's, and DOK is the amount of depth of thinking that must occur. We want rigor, and thus, we want complexity in our teachings.

Bloom's Taxonomy	Webb's Depth of Knowledge
Knowledge/Remembering The recall of specifics and universals, involving little more than bringing to mind the appropriate material.	**Recall** The recall of a fact, information, or procedure (e.g., What are three critical-skill cues for the overhand throw?).
Comprehension/Understanding The ability to process knowledge on a low level such that the knowledge can be reproduced or communicated without a verbatim repetition.	**Skill/Concept** The use of information, conceptual knowledge, procedures, two or more steps, etc.
Application/Applying The ability to use information in another familiar situation.	**Strategy Thinking** Requires reasoning, developing a plan, or sequence of steps; has some complexity; more than one possible answer.
Analysis/Analyzing The ability to break information into parts to explore understandings and relationships.	**Extended Thinking** Requires an investigation as well as time to think and process multiple conditions of the problem or task.
Synthesis and Evaluation/Evaluating and Creating Putting together elements and parts to form a whole and then making value judgements about the method.	

Adapted from Wyoming School Health and Physical Education (2001)

Correlation to the Standards

Shell Education is committed to producing educational materials that are research and standards based. In this effort, we have correlated all of our products to the academic standards of all 50 states, the District of Columbia, the Department of Defense Dependents Schools, and all Canadian provinces.

How to Find Standards Correlations

To print a customized correlation report of this product for your state, visit our website at http://www.shelleducation.com and follow the on-screen directions. If you require assistance in printing correlation reports, please contact our Customer Service department at 1-877-777-3450.

Purpose and Intent of Standards

Legislation mandates that all states adopt academic standards that identify the skills students will learn in kindergarten through grade twelve. Many states also have standards for Pre–K. This same legislation sets requirements to ensure the standards are detailed and comprehensive.

Standards are designed to focus instruction and guide adoption of curricula. Standards are statements that describe the criteria necessary for students to meet specific academic goals. They define the knowledge, skills, and content students should acquire at each level. Standards are also used to develop standardized tests to evaluate students' academic progress. Teachers are required to demonstrate how their lessons meet state standards. State standards are used in the development of all of our products, so educators can be assured they meet the academic requirements of each state.

Common Core State Standards

Many lessons in this book are aligned to the Common Core State Standards (CCSS). The standards support the objectives presented throughout the lessons and are provided on the Digital Resource CD (filename: standards.pdf).

TESOL and WIDA Standards

The lessons in this book promote English language development for English language learners. The standards listed on the Digital Resource CD (filename: standards.pdf) support the language objectives presented throughout the lessons.

Standards Chart

Common Core State Standard	Lesson(s)
Language.5.1.a—Explain the function of conjunctions, prepositions, and interjections in general and their function in particular sentences	Parts of Speech p. 119
Language.5.4.b—Use common grade-appropriate Greek and Latin affixes and roots as clues to the meaning of a word	Connecting with Affixes and Roots p. 29
Language.5.5—Demonstrate understanding of figurative language, word relationships, and nuances in word meanings	Shades of Meaning Accordion p. 140
Language.5.5.a—Interpret figurative language, including similes and metaphors, in context	Let's Study Figurative Language p. 146
Reading: Literature.5.5—Explain how a series of chapters, scenes, or stanzas fits together to provide the overall structure of a particular story, drama, or poem	That's the Order p. 129
Reading: Literature.5.6—Describe how a narrator's or speaker's point of view influences how events are described	Evidence to Support Point of View p. 116
Reading: Informational Text.5.5—Compare and contrast the overall structure (e.g., chronology, comparison, cause/effect, problem/solution) of events, ideas, concepts, or information in two or more texts	Resource Comparison p. 73
Writing.5.2.a—Introduce a topic clearly, provide a general observation and focus, and group related information logically; include formatting (e.g., headings), illustrations, and multimedia when useful to aiding comprehension	Support That Statement p. 106
Writing.5.2.d—Use precise language and domain-specific vocabulary to inform about or explain the topic	Noticing Nouns p. 47
Writing.5.3.c—Use a variety of transitional words, phrases, and clauses to manage the sequence of events	Transitional Phrases p. 76
Writing.5.5—With guidance and support from peers and adults, develop and strengthen writing as needed by planning, revising, editing, rewriting, or trying a new approach	Evaluating Revisions p. 66

Standards Chart *(cont.)*

Common Core State Standard	Lesson(s)
Math.5.A.2—Write simple expressions that record calculations with numbers and interpret numerical expressions without evaluating them. For example, express the calculation "add 8 and 7, then multiply by 2" as $2 \times (8 + 7)$. Recognize that $3 \times (18932 + 921)$ is three times as large as $18932 + 921$, without having to calculate the indicated sum or product	Expression Einsteins p. 60
Math.5.G.3—Understand that attributes belonging to a category of two-dimensional figures also belong to all subcategories of that category. For example, all rectangles have four right angles, and squares are rectangles, so all squares have four right angles	Comparing 2-D Shapes p. 70
Math.5.MD.1—Convert among different-sized standard measurement units within a given measurement system (e.g., convert 5 cm to 0.05 m) and use these conversions in solving multi-step, real world problems	Convert It p. 131
Math.5.MD.3—Recognize volume as an attribute of solid figures and understand concepts of volume measurement	Connecting with Volume p. 43
Math.5.NF.1—Add and subtract fractions with unlike denominators (including mixed numbers) by replacing given fractions with equivalent fractions in such a way as to produce an equivalent sum or difference of fractions with like denominators	Replacing with Equivalent Fractions p. 142

McREL Standard	Lesson(s)
Science 6.1—Knows the organization of simple food chains and food webs (e.g., green plants make their own food with sunlight, water, and air; some animals eat the plants; some animals eat the animals that eat the plants)	Food Chain Accordion p. 137
Science 8.1—Knows that matter has different states (i.e., solid, liquid, gas) and that each state has distinct physical properties; some common materials such as water can be changed from one state to another by heating or cooling	Let's Study Water Forms p. 144

Standards Chart *(cont.)*

McREL Standard	Lesson(s)
Science 9.3—Knows that light can be reflected, refracted, or absorbed	Light Examples p. 96
Science 11.2—Knows that good scientific explanations are based on evidence (observations) and scientific knowledge	Overtly Observant p. 63
History 2.2—Understands that specific individuals had a great impact on history	Historical Contributions p. 94
Civics 9.3—Knows how specific documents in American history set forth shared values, principles, and beliefs	Connecting with the Bill of Rights p. 35
Civics 15.1—Understands that the Constitution is a written document which states that the fundamental purposes of American government are to protect individual rights and promote the common good	Origin of Our Rights p. 109
Civics 15.3—Knows that the government was created by people who had the following beliefs: the government is established by and for the people, the people have the right to choose their representatives, and the people have the right to change their government and the Constitution	Amending the Constitution p. 127
Geography 2.1—Knows major physical and human features of places as they are represented on maps and globes	Geography Gurus p. 54

TESOL and WIDA Standard	Lesson(s)
English language learners **communicate** for **social**, **intercultural**, and **instructional** purposes within the school setting	All lessons
English language learners **communicate** information, ideas, and concepts necessary for academic success in the area of **language arts**	All lessons

Content Area Correlations Chart

Content Area	Lessons
Reading 📖	Connecting with Affixes and Roots p. 29; Resource Comparison p. 73; Evidence to Support Point of View p. 116; That's the Order p. 129; Shades of Meaning Accordion p. 140; Let's Study Figurative Language p. 146
Writing ✏️	Noticing Nouns p. 47; Evaluating Revisions p. 66; Transitional Phrases p. 76; Support That Statement p. 106; Parts of Speech p. 119
Math 🖩	Connecting with Volume p. 43; Expression Einsteins p. 60; Comparing 2-D Shapes p. 70; Convert It p. 131; Replacing with Equivalent Fractions p. 142
Social Studies 🌐	Connecting with the Bill of Rights p. 35; Geography Gurus p. 54; Historical Contributions p. 94; Origin of Our Rights p. 109; Amending the Constitution p. 127
Science ⚗️	Overtly Observant p. 63; Light Examples p. 96; Food Chain Accordion p. 137; Let's Study Water Forms p. 144

Connecting with Affixes and Roots

Brain-Powered Strategy	Standard
It's All About Me	Use common, grade-appropriate Greek and Latin affixes and roots as clues to the meaning of a word

Vocabulary Words	Materials
• affix • Greek • Latin • root	• *Affixes and Roots Cards* (pages 31–32) • *My Geode Connection* (page 33) • *Our Illustrations* (page 34) • sticky notes • dictionaries • chart paper • markers

Preparation Note: Prior to the lesson, cut apart the *Affixes and Roots Cards* (pages 31–32).

Procedures

Model

1. Display each of the affix and root cards on the board. Ask students to brainstorm words they know that contain each of the affixes and roots: *geo-*, *spec-*, *semi-*, *scrib-*, *inter-*, *audi-*, *lumen-*, and *dict-*. Write those words under the displayed cards.

2. Distribute eight sticky notes to each student. Have students write on the sticky notes what they think each Greek and Latin affix or root means and stick the notes by each corresponding card.

3. Model how to use a dictionary to look up an affix or root. Do this for the affix and root list by using the brainstormed list for *geo-*. Ask students what they know about the words to help them figure out what *geo-* means. Ask students to discuss with partners the connection between the words. Then, look up *geo-* in the dictionary and share that *geo-* means "earth" or "soil."

4. Tell students that they will be doing a strategy called *It's All About Me*. (For detailed information on this strategy, see page 12.)

Connecting with Affixes and Roots *(cont.)*

5. Tell students that they will create a movement for each prefix and then model a think-aloud for the word *geode*. For example: "*Geo*- means 'earth' or 'soil.' I know this from looking it up in the dictionary. When I think about the word *geode,* I can picture digging through the earth with a shovel or spade and coming across a roundish rock. I can imagine using my shovel to crack it open and seeing the gems inside." (Act out digging, finding a geode, and then cracking it open.)

6. Write *geo*- on the board, and draw a picture of a rock cracking open to reveal the root *geo*-. Explain your personal connection to the word *geode* such as seeing the beautiful rocks and stones at the natural history museum. Add details to your drawing to show, for example that it is in a museum display case. Distribute the *My Geode Connection* activity sheet (page 33) to students and have them add any words or illustrations they feel connect to the word *geode*.

Apply/Analyze

7. Arrange desks into seven stations and give each station a dictionary and one card from the *Affixes and Roots Cards* after you remove *geo*-. Divide students among the seven stations and have them choose partners to work with.

8. With their partners, have students use the affixes or roots at their stations to create movements that visually capture the meanings of the prefixes, as was done previously as a class. Encourage students to relate the prefix to something personal.

9. Instruct students to work independently to turn the definition of the affix or root into an illustration that captures the meaning or makes a personal connection.

10. Divide students into small groups. Distribute a sheet of chart paper and markers to each group. Ask students to record their illustrations on their chart paper.

Evaluate/Create

11. Have students rotate from station to station discussing the various affixes and roots illustrations. As they view the illustrations, have students keep the following questions in mind:

- What is the affix or root?

- How accurately did your classmates capture the meaning of the affix or root? Explain.

- Is there something you would add or change to capture the meaning in a different way or to make it more meaningful to you?

12. Distribute the *Our Illustrations* activity sheet (page 34) to students. Have students work with partners to replicate pictures that someone at each group illustrated in the left box of their activity sheets. Underneath, have students write details that describe the affix or root.

13. Working independently, instruct each student to create his or her own illustration in the boxes on the right side of their activity sheet. If they choose, students can combine (synthesize) illustrations from their peers. Have them record an explanation about each affix or root below their illustrations.

Affixes and Roots Cards

Teacher Directions: Cut apart the cards below.

geo-

spec-

inter-

semi-

Affixes and Roots Cards *(cont.)*

audi-

dict-

lumen-

scrib-

Name: _____   Date: _____

My Geode Connection

Directions: Add something to the picture that illustrates a personal connection you have made to the word *geode*.

Name: _____   Date: _____

Our Illustrations

Directions: Write the words your teacher gives you below. Draw pictures of your classmates' illustrations in the left column. Below each picture, explain what you drew. Then, draw and describe your own illustrations in the right column.

Group Illustrations	My Illustrations
Word:	
_____	_____
_____	_____
Word:	
_____	_____
_____	_____

Connecting with the Bill of Rights

Brain-Powered Strategy	Standard
It's All About Me	Knows how specific documents in American history set forth shared values, principles, and beliefs

Vocabulary Words

- beliefs
- Bill of Rights
- principles
- values

Materials

- *Bill of Rights Cards* (pages 37–41)
- *My First Amendment Connection* (page 42)
- *Our Illustrations* (page 34)
- sticky notes
- chart paper
- markers
- newspaper article relating to individual rights

Preparation Note: Prior to the lesson, cut apart the *Bill of Rights Cards* (pages 37–41).

Procedures

Model

1. Display each of the *Bill of Rights Cards* on the board. Ask students to brainstorm a list of actions or behaviors that are protected by each of the amendments.

2. Distribute sticky notes to students. Have each student write on a sticky note a phrase that summarizes the amendment and stick the notes by each corresponding card.

amendment · · ·

3. Explain to students the history of the Bill of Rights and how some people felt that the Constitution didn't provide enough detail about individual protections. Explain how individual states wrote their own declarations of rights prior to ratifying the United States Constitution. Discuss how these declarations of rights inspired the first 10 amendments to the United States Constitution, called the *Federal Bill of Rights*. Once the Federal Bill of Rights was adopted, it then influenced the texts of the individual state constitutions.

4. Tell students that they will be doing a strategy called *It's All About Me*. (For detailed information on this strategy, see page 12.)

Connecting with the Bill of Rights *(cont.)*

5. Write the first amendment on the board, and draw a picture of something that relates to it. Explain how the drawing is your personal connection to the amendment. Add details to your drawing. Distribute copies of the *My First Amendment Connection* activity sheet (page 42) to students and have them add any words or illustrations they feel connect to the first amendment.

Apply/Analyze

6. Arrange desks into nine stations and give each station a different amendment, distributing to each a single *Bill of Rights Card*. Divide students among the nine stations and have them choose partners to work with.

7. Working with their partners, have students use the *Bill of Rights Card* at each station to create movements that visually capture the meaning of the amendment. Encourage students to relate the amendment to something personal.

8. Instruct students to work independently to turn the meaning of the amendment into an illustration that captures the meaning or makes a personal connection.

9. Divide students into small groups again. Distribute a sheet of chart paper and markers to each group. Ask students to record their illustrations on their chart paper.

Evaluate/Create

10. Have students rotate from station to station discussing the various amendments and their illustrations. As they view the illustrations, have students keep the following questions in mind:

- Can you figure out how the wording of the amendment relates to the illustration?

- How did your classmates capture the meaning of the amendment?

- Is there something you would add or change to capture the meaning in a different way or to make it more meaningful to you?

11. Distribute copies of the *Our Illustrations* activity sheet (page 34) to students. Have students work with partners to draw pictures that someone at each group illustrated in the left box of their activity sheets. Underneath, have students write details that describe the amendment.

12. Working independently, instruct each student to create his or her own illustration in the box on the right side of his or her activity sheet. If they choose, students can synthesize illustrations from their peers. Have them record an explanation about each amendment below their illustrations.

13. Provide students with a recent newspaper article relating to individual rights protected by the Bill of Rights. Have students choose and defend how the text relates to specific rights and evaluate if the action should be protected. For example, you may provide students with a newspaper article about people speaking out against a new law. Students can compose a statement that explains their positions on the law.

Bill of Rights Cards

Teacher Directions: Cut apart the cards below.

First Amendment: Congress shall make no law respecting an establishment of religion, or prohibiting the free exercise thereof; or abridging the freedom of speech, or of the press; or the right of the people peaceably to assemble, and to petition the government for a redress of grievances.

Second Amendment: A well-regulated militia, being necessary to the security of a free state, the right of the people to keep and bear arms, shall not be infringed.

Bill of Rights Cards (cont.)

Third Amendment: No soldier shall, in time of peace be quartered in any house, without the consent of the owner, nor in time of war, but in a manner to be prescribed by law.

Fourth Amendment: The right of the people to be secure in their persons, houses, papers, and effects, against unreasonable searches and seizures, shall not be violated, and no warrants shall issue, but upon probable cause, supported by oath or affirmation, and particularly describing the place to be searched, and the persons or things to be seized.

Bill of Rights Cards *(cont.)*

Fifth Amendment: No person shall be held to answer for a capital, or otherwise infamous crime, unless on a presentment or indictment of a grand jury, except in cases arising in the land or naval forces, or in the militia, when in actual service in time of war or public danger; nor shall any person be subject for the same offense to be twice put in jeopardy of life or limb; nor shall be compelled in any criminal case to be a witness against himself, nor be deprived of life, liberty, or property, without due process of law; nor shall private property be taken for public use, without just compensation.

Sixth Amendment: In all criminal prosecutions, the accused shall enjoy the right to a speedy and public trial, by an impartial jury of the state and district wherein the crime shall have been committed, which district shall have been previously ascertained by law, and to be informed of the nature and cause of the accusation; to be confronted with the witnesses against him; to have compulsory process for obtaining witnesses in his favor, and to have the assistance of counsel for his defense.

Bill of Rights Cards (cont.)

Seventh Amendment: In suits at common law, where the value in controversy shall exceed twenty dollars, the right of trial by jury shall be preserved, and no fact tried by a jury, shall be otherwise reexamined in any court of the United States, than according to the rules of the common law.

Eighth Amendment: Excessive bail shall not be required, nor excessive fines imposed, nor cruel and unusual punishments inflicted.

Bill of Rights Cards *(cont.)*

Ninth Amendment: The enumeration in the Constitution, of certain rights, shall not be construed to deny or disparage others retained by the people.

Tenth Amendment: The powers not delegated to the United States by the Constitution, nor prohibited by it to the states, are reserved to the states respectively, or to the people.

Name: _____ Date: _____

My First Amendment Connection

Directions: Add something to the picture that illustrates a personal connection you have made to the First Amendment. Then, describe your picture.

Connecting with Volume

Brain-Powered Strategy	**Standard**
It's All About Me	Recognize volume as an attribute of solid figures and understand concepts of volume measurement

Vocabulary Words

- attribute
- height
- length
- solid figures
- volume
- width

Materials

- *Volume Cards* (pages 45–46)
- *Our Illustrations* (page 34)
- *Millions to Measure* by David M. Schwartz
- realia or pictures of various irregular-shaped solid figures
- chart paper
- markers
- text sample mentioning volume

Preparation Note: Prior to the lesson, cut apart the *Volume Cards* (pages 45–46).

Procedures

Model

1. Read the book *Millions to Measure* aloud. Discuss determining volume with students.

2. Show examples of different solid figures. Provide time for students to look at each one and comment to one another how they would go about determining its volume. Explain that these shapes are difficult to determine the volume of because they have an irregular shape. Tell students that common figures, like a cube, sphere, cylinder, cone, and pyramid all have formulas that can help determine the volume.

3. On the board write the word *cube* and the formula *length × width × height*. Share a story about your own experience determining the volume of a cube or box. Show an example of a movement for remembering the formula by pretending to hold a box and trace the length, the width, and then the height of the cube to determine how much it will hold.

4. Tell students the following story: "I remember when I was looking for something to hold all the baseballs we use at practice. I was looking for a box that could be easily stacked in the garage, and I knew I needed it to hold at least 25 baseballs. I knew that a baseball was about 3 inches in diameter. I found a box that was 9 inches wide, 12 inches long, and 9 inches high. Because I could determine the volume of the box, I knew that it would hold at least the 25 baseballs that I had to store."

Connecting with Volume *(cont.)*

5. Tell students that they will be doing a strategy called *It's All About Me*. (For detailed information on this strategy, see page 12.)

6. Show the *Volume Card* for the cube and ask, "How can the movement I made for determining the volume of the cube help me remember the equation?"

7. Model a drawing that either captures the experience just described or makes a picture representing the equation to find the volume of a cube.

8. Ask students to think about each equation for determining the volume of common shapes and relate it to something they know.

Apply/Analyze

9. Arrange desks into five stations and give each station a different *Volume Card*. Divide students among the stations and then have them choose partners.

10. Working with their partners, have students use their *Volume Card* to create movements, use the word to make a picture, or create an illustration that captures the memory that relates to that equation.

11. Instruct students to work independently to turn the meaning of the term into an illustration that captures the meaning or makes a personal connection.

12. Divide students into small groups. Distribute a sheet of chart paper and markers to each group. Ask students to record their illustrations on their chart papers. They should write the name of the solid figure and its equation on the back of the chart paper.

Evaluate/Create

13. Have students rotate from station to station discussing the various shapes and their illustrations. As they view the illustrations, have students keep the following questions in mind:

- What is the solid figure/equation represented?

- How can you identify how your classmates captured the meaning?

- Is there something you would add or change to capture the meaning in a different way or to make it more meaningful to you?

14. Distribute the *Our Illustrations* activity sheet (page 34) to students. Have students work with partners to draw pictures that someone at each group illustrated in the left box of their activity sheets. Underneath, have students write details.

15. Working independently, instruct each student to create his or her own illustration in the box in the right side of the activity sheet. If students choose, they can synthesize illustrations from their peers. Have them record an explanation about each figure or equation below their illustration.

16. Provide each student with a text mentioning volume such as a newspaper article about gas prices, a scientific paper, or a recipe. Have students choose and defend how the text relates to determining volume. Ask students to paraphrase to explain how the text relates to volume.

Volume Cards

Teacher Directions: Cut apart the cards below.

cube

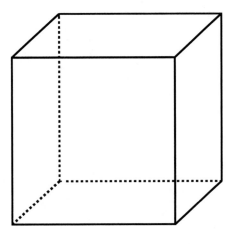

side × side × side

rectangular prism

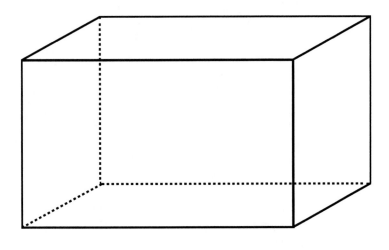

length × width × height

Volume Cards *(cont.)*

cylinder

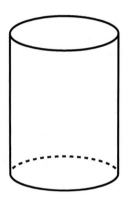

π *× radius² × height*

pyramid

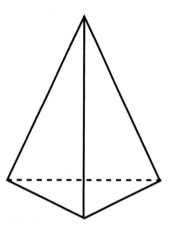

$\frac{1}{3}$ *× base × height*

Noticing Nouns

Brain-Powered Strategy	Standard
ABC Professors	Use precise language and domain-specific vocabulary to inform about or explain the topic

Vocabulary Words

- domain-specific vocabulary
- precise language
- robust
- substitute

Materials

- *Noun Partner Cards* (pages 49–52)
- *ABC Professor Notes* (page 53)
- writing paper
- chart paper
- reading texts

Preparation Note: Prior to the lesson, cut apart the *Noun Partner Cards* (pages 49–52).

Procedures

Model

1. Distribute a *Noun Partner Card* to students. Without talking, have them find their matching nouns and sit with that partner. Each student should find only one partner, even though there may be more than two cards per noun distributed among students.

2. Distribute writing paper to students. Tell students that they will each have three minutes to think of other nouns that are associated with the noun they have been given. For example, if they have the noun *kitchen,* students may brainstorm a list including the nouns *spoon, plate, platter,* and *whisk.*

3. Direct student groups to then sort their noun lists into two categories: *specific nouns* and *general nouns.* Discuss how specific nouns help create an image and help the readers visualize what the author is describing. Once students have finished sorting, have them share a few general and specific nouns with the class.

4. Inform each student that they are now "Noun Experts" because they understand the function of strong, descriptive nouns.

5. Tell students that they will be doing a strategy called *ABC Professors.* (For detailed information on this strategy, see page 13.)

Noticing Nouns *(cont.)*

6. Create a replica of the *ABC Professor Notes* activity sheet (page 53) on the board or on a sheet of chart paper. Model putting a strong, descriptive noun or noun phrase in each box that begins with that letter. For example, in the *V* box you may write *veterinarian*. In the *F* box, *falcon* may be written. Have students help complete three more boxes.

7. Invite a student to come to the front of the class to model reading the notes. Read the word or phrase in letter box *A* from the chart created, emphasizing the word that begins with the letter *A*. Have students read the word or phrase for the letter *B* and continue to take turns, as needed.

Apply/Analyze

8. Divide students into pairs and distribute the *ABC Professor Notes* activity sheet to each pair. Have each student pair complete it with words or phrases that demonstrate their understanding of strong and descriptive nouns.

Evaluate/Create

9. Invite a pair of students to come to the front of the class and model how to share responses and provide positive feedback. Then, combine pairs to make groups of four.

10. Instruct students to discuss their responses, sharing what they have written for some letters and providing positive feedback for one another's answers. They can record new nouns or noun phrases they did not have that were shared by others.

11. Have students return to their original pairs and provide them with a second *ABC Professor Notes* activity sheet. Instruct students to complete the activity a second time, but this time add depth by also adding an adjective or verb to the nouns to add more description and put the words in the form of a question. For example, for the letter *V,* a student may write: *Why was the **v**eterinarian **v**ivacious?*

12. As students begin to master this technique, walk them through Bloom's Revised Taxonomy and guide them through the use of question stems. For additional support on Bloom's Taxonomy, see page 23.

13. Provide students with multiple texts demonstrating the use of strong, descriptive nouns to read. As a whole class, analyze and evaluate the authors' use of nouns. Discuss the similarities and differences between informational and narrative texts.

Noun Partner Cards

Teacher Directions: Cut apart the cards below.

living room

car

baseball

beach

Noun Partner Cards *(cont.)*

grass

dog

desk

road

Noun Partner Cards *(cont.)*

library

shoe

music

carrot

Noun Partner Cards *(cont.)*

office

chair

dining room

couch

#51182—*Brain-Powered Lessons to Engage All Learners* © *Shell Education*

Name: _____   Date: _____

ABC Professor Notes

Directions: Think of a descriptive noun. What letter does that word begin with? Find that box and write or draw the word in the box.

A	B	C	D	E
F	G	H	I	J
K	L	M	N	O
P	Q	R	S	T
U	V	W	X	Y
Z				

Geography Gurus

Brain-Powered Strategy	Standard
ABC Professors	Knows major physical and human features of places as they are represented on maps and globes

Vocabulary Words

- bay
- canyon
- continent
- equator
- inlet

Materials

- *Geography Cards* (pages 56–58)
- *ABC Professor Notes* (page 59)
- writing paper
- chart paper
- maps, atlases, globes

Preparation Note: Prior to the lesson, cut apart the *Geography Cards* (pages 56–58).

Procedures

Model

1. Provide each student with a *Geography Card*. Without talking, have them all find a matching geography term and sit with one partner. Each student should find only one partner even though there may be more than two cards per term distributed among students.

2. Distribute writing paper to students. Tell students that they will each have five minutes to create a labeled visual representation of their geography term. They must consider what is around it, where it might be located, and even create a name. Once students have completed this, have them share their ideas with the class.

3. Inform students that they are now "Geography Gurus" because they are now the experts.

4. Tell students that they will be doing a strategy called *ABC Professors*. (For detailed information on this strategy, see page 13.)

5. Create a replica of the activity sheet *ABC Professor Notes* (page 59) on the board or on a sheet of chart paper. Model putting a geography word, phrase, or fact in each box that begins with the corresponding letter. For example, in the *R* box, you may write *river*. In the *P* box, *peninsula* may be written. Have students help complete three more boxes.

6. Invite a student to come to the front of the class to model reading the notes. Read the word or phrase in the letter box *A* from the chart created, emphasizing the word that begins with the letter *A*. Have students read the word or phrase for the letter *B* and continue to take turns, as needed.

Geography Gurus *(cont.)*

Apply/Analyze

7. Divide students into pairs and distribute the *ABC Professor Notes* activity sheet to each pair. Have them complete it with words or phrases related to geography.

Evaluate/Create

8. Invite a pair of students to come to the front of the class and model how to share responses and provide positive feedback. Then, combine pairs to make groups of four.

9. Instruct students to discuss their responses, sharing what they have written for some letters and providing positive feedback for one another's answers. They can record new geography words or phrases they did not have that were shared by others.

10. Have students return to their original pairs and provide them with a second *ABC Professor Notes* activity sheet. Instruct students to complete the activity a second time, but this time add depth by putting the content into a question format. Tell them that a student asks a question that answers the previous student's question or relates to what was stated. Each response a student gives must start with the next letter of the alphabet. For example:

Student A: **A**tlases show what?

Student B: **B**oundaries between states and countries. What is a state?

Student C: **C**an we define a state by saying it is a territory of land within a country?

11. As students begin to master this technique, walk them through Bloom's Revised Taxonomy, and guide them through the use of question stems. For additional support on Bloom's Taxonomy, see page 23.

12. Provide students with multiple maps, atlases, and globes. As a class, categorize how and where each of the geography terms is represented.

13. Provide students with three or four geography terms and ask them to construct a map or atlas representing a fictional location using the terms.

Geography Cards

Teacher Directions: Cut apart the cards below.

island

continent

equator

inlet

Geography Cards *(cont.)*

bay

canyon

ocean

wetlands

Geography Cards *(cont.)*

lines of latitude

compass rose

tributary

pole

Name: _____ Date: _____

ABC Professor Notes

Directions: Think of something that relates to the topic of geography. What letter does that word begin with? Find that box and write or draw the word in the box.

A	B	C	D	E
F	G	H	I	J
K	L	M	N	O
P	Q	R	S	T
U	V	W	X	Y
Z				

Expression Einsteins

Brain-Powered Strategy	Standard
ABC Professors	Write simple expressions that record calculations with numbers and interpret numerical expressions without evaluating them

Vocabulary Words

- bracket
- evaluate
- expression
- parenthesis

Materials

- *ABC Professor Notes* (page 62)
- writing paper
- chart paper
- informational text about simplifying expressions

Procedures

Model

1. Distribute writing paper to students. Randomly provide each student with a numerical expression. Have each student write the numerical expression on his or her sheet of paper. Without talking, have each student find five classmates with different expressions to form a group.

2. Distribute a sheet of writing paper to each group. Tell students that they will each have five minutes to work together to place the expressions in order from least to greatest.

3. When time is up, have students share how they may have interpreted the expressions and determined a relative value without solving them. Inform students that they are now "Expression Einsteins" because they are the experts.

4. Tell students that they will be doing a strategy called *ABC Professors*. (For detailed information on this strategy, see page 13.)

5. Create a replica of the *ABC Professor Notes* activity sheet (page 62) on the board or on a sheet of chart paper. Model putting a word, phrase, or fact in each box that begins with the corresponding letter. For example, in the *P* box, you may write *parenthesis*. In the *B* box, *bracket* may be written. Have students help complete three more boxes.

6. Invite a student to come to the front of the class to model reading the notes. Read the word or phrase in the letter box *A* from the chart created, emphasizing the word that begins with the letter *A*. Have students read the word or phrase for the letter *B* and continue to take turns, as needed.

Expression Einsteins (cont.)

Apply/Analyze

7. Divide students into pairs and distribute the *ABC Professor Notes* activity sheet to each pair. Have them complete it with words or phrases related to interpreting or simplifying expressions using the order of operations.

Evaluate/Create

8. Invite a pair of students to come to the front of the class and model how to share responses and provide positive feedback. Then, combine pairs to make groups of four.

9. Instruct students to discuss their responses, sharing what they have written for some letters and providing positive feedback for one another's answers. They can record new words or phrases they did not have that were shared by others.

10. Have students return to their original pairs and provide them with a second *ABC Professor Notes* activity sheet. Instruct students to complete the activity a second time, but this time, add depth by putting the content into a question format. Tell them that a student asks a question that answers the previous student's question or relates to what was stated. Each response a student gives must start with the next letter of the alphabet. For example:

Student A: *A* numerical expression is what?

Student B: *Basically*, it is a phrase that has numbers, operations, and/or variables. What is a variable?

Student C: *Can* we define a variable by saying it is the opposite of a constant?

11. As students begin to master this technique, walk them through Bloom's Revised Taxonomy and guide them through the use of question stems. For additional support on Bloom's Taxonomy, see page 23.

12. Provide students with multiple informational texts about simplifying expressions using the order of operations such as a page from a math textbook or an Internet article. Either independently or in pairs, have students synthesize the information and create a flow chart explaining how to simplify expressions using the order of operations and using the words from their *ABC Professor Notes* activity sheets.

Name: _____   Date: _____

ABC Professor Notes

Directions: Think of something that relates to the topic your teacher gave you. What letter does that word begin with? Find that box and write or draw the word in the box.

A	B	C	D	E
F	G	H	I	J
K	L	M	N	O
P	Q	R	S	T
U	V	W	X	Y
Z				

Overtly Observant

Brain-Powered Strategy	Standard
ABC Professors	Knows that good scientific explanations are based on evidence (observations) and scientific knowledge

Vocabulary Words	Materials
• scientific evidence • scientific explanation • scientific knowledge	• *ABC Professor Notes* (page 65) • writing paper • chart paper • informational texts about observations of a scientific object

Procedures

Model

1. Distribute writing paper to students. Randomly provide each student with a scientific statement based on what you have been studying and have each student copy the given statement on his or her sheet of paper. For example, if you have been studying the solar system, a statement might be: *The Earth orbits around the sun.* Without talking, have each student find five classmates with different statements to form a group.

2. Distribute writing paper to students. Tell students that they will have five minutes to work together to design an experiment that would test their scientific statement. In the example above, students could take a rocket ship into space and observe Earth and the sun to observe Earth's orbit.

3. When time is up, have students share how they could test the scientific statement. Discuss or review the idea that it is important to create an experiment that allows you to observe a single object.

4. Tell students that they will be doing a strategy called *ABC Professors*. (For detailed information on this strategy, see page 13.)

5. Create a replica of the *ABC Professor Notes* activity sheet (page 65) on the board or on a sheet of chart paper. Model putting a word, a phrase, or a fact about the scientific process in each box that begins with the corresponding letter. For example, in the *P* box, you may write *predict*. In the *B* box, *biologists observe living organisms* may be written. Have students help complete three more boxes.

6. Invite a student to come to the front of the class to model reading the notes. Read the word or phrase in the letter box *A* from the chart created, emphasizing the word that begins with the letter *A*. Have students read the word or phrase for the letter *B* and continue to take turns, as needed.

Overtly Observant *(cont.)*

Apply/Analyze

7. Divide students into pairs and distribute the *ABC Professor Notes* activity sheet to each pair. Have them complete it with words or phrases related to selected scientific statements.

Evaluate/Create

8. Invite a pair of students to come to the front of the class and model how to share responses and provide positive feedback. Then, combine pairs to make groups of four.

9. Instruct students to discuss their responses, sharing what they have written for some letters and providing positive feedback for one another's answers. They can record new science words or phrases they did not have that were shared by others.

10. Have students return to their original pairs and provide them with a second *ABC Professor Notes* activity sheet. Instruct students to complete the activity a second time, but this time add depth by putting the content into a question format. Tell them that a student asks a question that answers the previous student's question or relates to what was stated. Each response a student gives must start with the next letter of the alphabet. For example:

Student A: **A***sking* a question is the first step in the scientific process. Why?

Student B: **B***ecause* it helps you determine what you are trying to solve or find out. What is the next step?

Student C: **C***onducting* research is the second step. Where can I look for research?

11. As students begin to master this technique, walk them through Bloom's Revised Taxonomy, and guide them through the use of question stems. For additional support on Bloom's Taxonomy, see page 23.

12. Provide students with multiple informational texts about observations of a single object such as a page from a science textbook, a log of a scientific observation, or an Internet article. Either independently or in pairs, have students synthesize the information and create a flow chart explaining how to design a valid scientific observation using the words from their ABC Professor Notes.

13. Ask students to generate a statement synthesizing the information they learned about observations of a single subject with the help of their activity sheets.

Name: _____   Date: _____

ABC Professor Notes

Directions: Think of something that relates to the topic your teacher gave you. What letter does that word begin with? Find that box and write or draw the word in the box.

A	B	C	D	E
F	G	H	I	J
K	L	M	N	O
P	Q	R	S	T
U	V	W	X	Y
Z				

Evaluating Revisions

Brain-Powered Strategy	Standard
It Takes Two	With guidance and support from peers and adults, develop and strengthen writing as needed by planning, revising, editing, rewriting, or trying a new approach

Vocabulary Words

- editing
- planning
- revision

Materials

- *Compare and Contrast Revisions* (page 68)
- *Our Feedback* (page 69)
- chart paper
- two different colors of sticky notes
- student writing and revised samples

Preparation Note: Prior to the lesson, create a two-column T-chart on a sheet of chart paper. Write *Similarities* in the left column and *Differences* in the right column.

Procedures

Model

1. Write the following two versions of the same sentence on the board:

    - Version 1: The dog walked along the beach.

    - Version 2: One foggy morning, the dog crawled along the beach sniffing for starfish.

2. Tell students that they will be doing a strategy called *It Takes Two*. (For detailed information on this strategy, see page 14.)

3. Distribute two sticky notes to each student. Divide students into groups of four and ask them to compare the two sentences by recording a similarity on one and a difference on the other.

4. Model for students how to place the sticky notes on the chart in the appropriate columns. Have students practice placing the sticky notes they create on the chart.

5. Discuss the placement of the sticky notes and ask students to consider if any of the sticky notes should be moved. If so, why?

Evaluating Revisions *(cont.)*

Apply/Analyze

6. Divide students into four groups. Provide each group with a different piece of student writing and its revision. Have a student in each group read the piece aloud.

7. Distribute the *Compare and Contrast Revisions* activity sheet (page 68) to each group as well as two stacks of sticky notes (two different colors—one for each column).

8. Have students discuss the revisions and record their ideas, one per sticky note, and place them in the appropriate column on their *Compare and Contrast Revisions* activity sheet. Have students continue until the designated time is up or the task is considered complete.

Evaluate/Create

9. Have groups stand, leaving their activity sheets at their desks. At your signal, have groups rotate clockwise and sit to examine another group's chart.

10. Distribute the *Our Feedback* activity sheet (page 69) to each group. Allow students time to analyze another group's work and complete the activity sheet. If there are disagreements or recommendations for changes, students should note the difference on a different colored sticky note to add to a deeper discussion. Students should consider the following questions:

- Do you agree or disagree with your classmates' choices? Explain.

- Do you feel the revisions the author made strengthened the writing? If so, how? If not, why?

- Would you recommend any additional revisions or changes that would strengthen the writing?

11. Allow groups to synthesize the feedback provided on their original activity sheets and make revisions as necessary. They should discuss as a group how their thinking has changed based on the feedback from others in the class.

12. Debrief with students and ask what they learned from the lesson.

13. Have students independently look at their own drafts and revisions to see if the revisions improved their focus and elaboration.

Name: _____ Date: _____

Compare and Contrast Revisions

Directions: After reading the draft and the revision, use sticky notes to write your ideas. Place each sticky note in the appropriate column.

Similarities	Differences

Our Feedback

Directions: Discuss another group's chart. Record your group's responses below.

What We Agree With, and Why	What We Disagree With, and Why

Comparing 2-D Shapes

Brain-Powered Strategy	**Standard**
It Takes Two	Understand that attributes belonging to a category of two-dimensional figures also belong to all subcategories of that category

Vocabulary Words

- angle
- attributes
- edges
- face
- symmetry

Materials

- *Comparing Two-Dimensional Shapes* (page 72)
- *Our Feedback* (page 69)
- chart paper
- two different colors of sticky notes
- informational texts related to two-dimensional shapes

Preparation Note: Prior to the lesson, create a two-column T-chart on a sheet of chart paper. Write *Similarities* in the left column and *Differences* in the right column.

Procedures

Model

1. Have students suggest two popular television shows. As a class, discuss what both shows are about.

2. Tell students that they will be doing a strategy called *It Takes Two*. (For detailed information on this strategy, see page 14.)

3. Distribute two sticky notes to each student. Divide students into groups of four and ask them to compare the two television programs by recording a similarity on one and a difference on the other.

4. Model for students how to place the sticky notes on the chart in the appropriate columns. Have students practice placing the sticky notes they create on the chart.

5. Discuss the placement of the sticky notes and ask students to consider if any of the sticky notes should be moved. If so, why?

Comparing 2-D Shapes *(cont.)*

Apply/Analyze

6. Divide students into four groups and then assign each group two different two-dimensional shapes.

7. Distribute the *Comparing Two-Dimensional Shapes* activity sheet (page 72) to each group as well as two stacks of sticky notes (two different colors—one for each column).

8. Have students discuss and record their ideas, one per sticky note, and place them in the appropriate column on their *Comparing Two-Dimensional Shapes* activity sheet. Have students continue until the designated time is up or the task is considered complete.

Evaluate/Create

9. Have groups stand, leaving their *Comparing Two-Dimensional Shapes* activity sheets at their desks. At your signal, have groups rotate clockwise and sit to examine another group's chart.

10. Distribute the *Our Feedback* activity sheet (page 69) to each group. Allow students time to discuss that group's work and complete the activity sheet. If there are disagreements or recommendations for changes, they should note the difference on a different colored sticky note to add to a deeper discussion. Students should consider the following questions:

- Do you agree or disagree with your classmates' choices?

- Are there any changes you would make?

11. Allow groups to synthesize the feedback provided on their original activity sheets and make revisions, as necessary. They should discuss as a group how their thinking has changed based on the feedback from others in the class.

12. Debrief with students and ask what they learned from the lesson.

13. Have students independently complete a comparison of two more two-dimensional shapes. As an alternative activity, have students combine groups with a group that has one similar shape.

14. Provide students with a variety of informational texts related to two-dimensional shapes. Ideas include a page from a textbook, an encyclopedia article, or a web page. Have students work either independently or in pairs to create a rule for each two-dimensional shape and its attributes. For example, students might say if a shape has four sides, right angles, and all sides are equal, it is a square; but if only the opposite sides are equal, then it is a rectangle.

Name: _____ Date: _____

Comparing Two-Dimensional Shapes

Directions: Listen to your teacher for the two shapes you will compare. Write them on the lines below. On sticky notes, write your ideas. Place each sticky note in the appropriate column.

_____ and _____

Similarities	Differences

Resource Comparison

Brain-Powered Strategy	Standard
It Takes Two	Compare and contrast the overall structure of events, ideas, concepts, or information in two or more texts

Vocabulary Words

- chronology
- events
- evidence
- resources

Materials

- *Comparing Resources* (page 75)
- *Our Feedback* (page 69)
- chart paper
- two different colors of sticky notes
- resources or research materials on the same topic from the Internet, books, or magazines

Preparation Note: Prior to the lesson, create a two-column T-chart on a sheet of chart paper. Write *Similarities* in the left column and *Differences* in the right column.

Procedures

Model

1. Have students suggest two different kinds of shoes. As a class, discuss features of each type of shoe. Then, record a similarity on one sticky note and record a difference on another.

2. Tell students that they will be doing a strategy called *It Takes Two*. (For detailed information on this strategy, see page 14.)

3. Distribute two sticky notes to each student. Divide students into groups of four, and ask them to compare the different kind of shoes by recording a similarity on one and a difference on the other.

4. Model for students how to place the sticky notes on the chart in the appropriate columns. Have students practice placing the sticky notes they create on the chart.

5. Discuss the placement of the sticky notes and ask students to consider if any of the sticky notes should be moved. If so, why?

Apply/Analyze

6. Divide students into four groups and then assign each group two different resources.

7. Distribute the *Comparing Resources* activity sheet (page 75) to each group, as well as two stacks of sticky notes (two different colors—one for each column).

8. Have students discuss and record their ideas, one per sticky note, and place them in the appropriate column on their *Comparing Resources* activity sheet. Have students continue until the designated time is up or the task is considered complete.

Resource Comparison *(cont.)*

Evaluate/Create

9. Have groups stand, leaving their *Comparing Resources* activity sheets at their desks. At your signal, have groups rotate clockwise and sit to examine another group's chart.

10. Distribute the *Our Feedback* activity sheet (page 69) to each group. Allow students time to discuss that group's work and complete the *Our Feedback* activity sheet. Students should consider the following questions:

- Do you agree or disagree with your classmates' choices?

- Are there any changes you would make?

If there are disagreements or recommendations for changes, they should note the difference on a different colored sticky note to add to a deeper discussion.

11. Allow groups to review the feedback provided on their original activity sheets and make recommendations, as necessary. They should discuss as a group how their thinking has changed based on the feedback from others in the class.

12. Debrief with students and ask what they learned from the lesson.

13. Have students work together to create a master class chart with everyone's sticky notes for the various resources. Make sure students read one another's notes and remove any duplicates.

14. Provide students with a variety of resources. Ask students to work in pairs or small groups to categorize and define the groups of resources.

15. After students have analyzed multiple resources, have them synthesize their findings by developing a list of rules for useful resources. Have students discuss the text features that make a resource useful.

Name: _____ Date: _____

Comparing Resources

∙∙

Directions: Listen to your teacher for the two resources you will compare. Write them on the lines below. On sticky notes, write your ideas. Place each sticky note in the appropriate column.

_____ and _____

Similarities	Differences

Transitional Phrases

Brain-Powered Strategy	Standard
Matchmaker	Use a variety of transitional words, phrases, and clauses to manage the sequence of events

Vocabulary Words

- clauses
- sequence of events
- transitional phrases
- transitional words

Materials

- *Types of Transitional Phrases Cards* (pages 78–81)
- *Transitional Phrases Cards* (pages 82–93)
- chart paper
- tape
- sample texts (fiction and nonfiction)

Preparation Note: Prior to the lesson, cut apart the *Types of Transitional Phrases Cards* (pages 78–81). There should be enough sets so that each student receives one card to wear. Additionally, cut apart the *Transitional Phrases Cards* (pages 82–93).

Procedures

Model

1. Discuss transitional phrases as a class. Work with students to brainstorm a list of transitional words. Ask, "Why do writers use transitional phrases?"

2. List student ideas on the board or on a sheet of chart paper. Make sure to highlight the idea that transitional phrases help readers and authors move from one idea to the other. They illustrate relationships, and they improve connections between thoughts.

3. Read a sample sentence aloud, leaving out the transitional phrase.

4. Ask students to identify the phrases from the board that would work with the sentence.

5. Discuss the merits of each, and as a class determine the best transition for the sample. Then, discuss the type of transition. Ask, "Does this transitional phrase illustrate an addition, consequence, contrast/comparison, direction, illustration, similarity, restatement, or sequence?"

6. Repeat Steps 3 through 5 with other samples until you are sure that students understand the activity.

7. Tell students that they will be doing a strategy called *Matchmaker*. (For detailed information on this strategy, see page 15.)

Transitional Phrases *(cont.)*

Apply/Analyze

8. Distribute a *Types of Transitional Phrases Card* to each student. Have students attach the cards to their shirts using tape. Then, divide students into groups of eight. Have them stand in a circle.

9. Place a set of *Transitional Phrases Cards* faceup on the floor in the center of each circle. Explain to students that they will hold hands and bend down to pick up a card, without grabbing their own. Without letting go, they will have to get the card they picked up to the correct person, according to his or her attached card. **Note**: For this version of the game, each label has three cards that match it.

10. Once students have completed one round, have them mix up the cards and try again, as time allows. Instruct students to not pick the same card they had before. In the last round, have students pick up the card that matches them.

Evaluate/Create

11. Place students in pairs. Have one partner begin by saying a sentence that has a transitional phrase. The other partner will listen to the sentence stated by his or her partner and explain why the transitional phrase makes sense in the sentence. Then, have partners discuss transitional phrases that would not make sense in the particular sentence.

12. Provide students with multiple fiction and nonfiction texts which use transitional phrases. Have students compare the transitional phrases used in each type of text. As a whole class, discuss and generalize the similarities and differences between the transitional phrases used in fiction versus nonfiction texts. For example, students might make the generalization that informational texts use temporal words more often than narrative texts.

Types of Transitional Phrases Cards

Teacher Directions: Cut apart the cards below.

illustration

details

Types of Transitional Phrases Cards *(cont.)*

concession

emphasis

Types of Transitional Phrases Cards *(cont.)*

addition

suggestion

Types of Transitional Phrases Cards *(cont.)*

time

space

Transitional Phrases Cards

Teacher Directions: Cut apart the cards below.

to illustrate

such as

Transitional Phrases Cards *(cont.)*

for instance

to enumerate

Transitional Phrases Cards *(cont.)*

in particular

in detail

#51182—*Brain-Powered Lessons to Engage All Learners*   © *Shell Education*

Transitional Phrases Cards (cont.)

above all

in fact

Transitional Phrases Cards *(cont.)*

of course

equally important

Transitional Phrases Cards *(cont.)*

not only

in the second place

Transitional Phrases Cards *(cont.)*

for this purpose

to this end

Transitional Phrases Cards *(cont.)*

with this in mind

in the meantime

Transitional Phrases Cards (cont.)

during the morning

at the same time

#51182—*Brain-Powered Lessons to Engage All Learners* © Shell Education

Transitional Phrases Cards *(cont.)*

in the forefront

in the distance

Transitional Phrases Cards (cont.)

in the background

at any rate

#51182—Brain-Powered Lessons to Engage All Learners

Transitional Phrases Cards (cont.)

even though

while it may be true

Historical Contributions

Brain-Powered Strategy	Standard
Matchmaker	Understands that specific individuals had a great impact on history

Vocabulary Words

- historical
- impact
- influence
- significant

Materials

- address labels
- index cards
- informational texts about historical figures
- chart paper

Preparation Note: Prior to the lesson, write the names of the historical figures you are studying on address labels. Write significant contributions for each person on index cards as well. Or you may wish to have students research the contributions. Make enough sets for each group to have one.

Procedures

Model

1. Tell students that they will be doing a strategy called *Matchmaker*. (For detailed information on this strategy, see page 15.)

2. Invite eight students to model the activity. Explain that each student will be wearing an address label with the name of a historical figure. Place all cards in the center of the circle. Instruct students to hold hands and bend down to randomly pick up an index card but not one that matches their own.

3. Explain to students that they are to read the contribution on the index card and, without letting go, get the card they picked up to the correct person, according to his or her address label. **Option:** You may choose not to have students hold hands and pick up a card; however, energy and engagement levels increase with the challenge of holding hands and not letting go.

4. Repeat Steps 2 and 3 with other samples until you are sure that students understand the activity.

Apply/Analyze

5. Divide students into groups of eight. Have them stand in a circle. Each student per group should be wearing an address label with the name of a different historical figure.

6. Place a set of index cards faceup on the floor in the center of each circle. Remind students that they are to hold hands and bend down to pick up an index card, without grabbing their own. Without letting go, they will have to get the card they picked up to the correct person, according to his or her address label.

Historical Contributions *(cont.)*

7. Once students have completed one round, have them mix up the cards and try again, as time allows. Instruct students to not pick the same card they had before. In the last round, have students pick up the cards that match themselves.

Evaluate/Create

8. Assign each student a different historical figure. Have each create an index card noting a significant accomplishment attributed to that figure to write on his or her index card. Play the game using new historical figures and the matching index cards.

9. Provide each student with an informational text about a historical figure to read independently. As a whole class, discuss the similarities and differences between the contributions, time period, and influence each figure had.

10. Create a classroom comparison chart on a sheet of chart paper comparing and contrasting the historical figures.

Light Examples

Brain-Powered Strategy	Standard
Matchmaker	Knows that light can be reflected, refracted, or absorbed

Vocabulary Words

- absorb
- reflect
- refract

Materials

- *Types of Light Energy Cards* (pages 98–99)
- *Light Examples Cards* (pages 100–105)
- address labels
- index cards
- informational text about energy being reflected, refracted, or absorbed

Preparation Note: Prior to the lesson, write the types of light energy on the address labels: *reflected*, *refracted*, or *absorbed*. Or you may wish to make copies and cut apart the *Types of Light Energy Cards* (pages 98–99). There should be enough sets so that each student receives one label to wear. Additionally, cut apart the *Light Examples Cards* (pages 100–105).

Procedures

Model

1. Review light energy and how light energy can be reflected, refracted, and absorbed by objects.

2. Tell students that they will be doing a strategy called *Matchmaker*. (For detailed information on this strategy, see page 15.)

3. Invite eight students to model the activity. Explain that each student will be wearing an address label stating either *reflected*, *refracted*, or *absorbed*. Place a single *Light Examples Card* faceup on the floor in front of each student. Instruct students to hold hands and bend down to pick up a *Light Examples Card,* without grabbing their own.

4. Explain to students that they are to read the item on the *Light Examples Cards* and, without letting go, get the card they picked up to the correct person, according to his or her address label in order to match if the object would reflect, refract, or absorb light energy. **Option:** You may choose not to have students hold hands and pick up a card; however, the energy and engagement levels increase with the challenge of holding hands and not letting go.

5. Repeat Steps 3 and 4 with other samples until you are sure that students understand the activity.

6. Discuss each match and, as a class, determine the best location for each sample.

Light Examples *(cont.)*

Apply/Analyze

7. Divide students into groups of eight. Have them stand in a circle. Each student should be wearing a different address label.

8. Place a set of *Light Examples Cards* faceup on the floor in the center of each circle. Explain to students that they will hold hands and bend down to pick up an index card, without grabbing their own. Without letting go, they will have to get the card they picked up to the correct person, according to the address label. **Note:** For this version of the game, each label has four cards that match it.

9. Once students have completed one round, have them mix up the cards and try again, as time allows. Instruct students to not pick the same cards they had before. In the last round, have students pick up the cards that match themselves.

Evaluate/Create

10. Ask student groups to brainstorm their own examples of objects for each address label. Write the examples on index cards and try again, as time allows.

11. Provide each student with an informational text about light being reflected, refracted, or absorbed. As a class, discuss the similarities and differences between each. Have students apply their understanding in a new way. Have students work in pairs or small groups to create a skit, a poem, or a chart synthesizing their knowledge about light.

Types of Light Energy Cards

Teacher Directions: Cut apart the cards below.

reflected

refracted

Types of Light Energy Cards *(cont.)*

absorbed

Light Examples Cards

Teacher Directions: Cut apart the cards below.

mirror

moon

Light Examples Cards (cont.)

snow

shiny aluminum foil

Light Examples Cards *(cont.)*

magnifying glass

prism

Light Examples Cards *(cont.)*

oil

diamonds

Light Examples Cards *(cont.)*

asphalt

dull metal

#51182—Brain-Powered Lessons to Engage All Learners

Light Examples Cards *(cont.)*

dark-colored car

matte photograph

Support That Statement

Brain-Powered Strategy	Standard
Just Say It	Introduce a topic clearly, provide a general observation and focus, and group related information logically; include formatting, illustrations, and multimedia when useful to aiding comprehension

Vocabulary Words	Materials
• focus • general observation • related information	• *Feedback Sheet* (page 108) • samples of student writing • chart paper

Preparation Note: Prior to the lesson, gather a sample of each student's writing.

Procedures

Model

1. Discuss the role of a thesis statement and supporting information in writing. Brainstorm as a class how and why it is important to have both a thesis statement and supporting information.

2. List student ideas on the board or on a sheet of chart paper. Make sure to highlight the ideas that a thesis statement helps readers know what you are trying to say, and supporting statements help readers understand why your thesis statement is valid.

3. Explain to students that they will focus on giving partners helpful feedback about their own writing. Read a sample paragraph.

4. Tell students that they will be doing a strategy called *Just Say It*. (For detailed information on this strategy, see page 16.)

5. Tell students that this strategy will help each of them hear feedback about his or her writing as a way to improve and strengthen his or her writing skills.

6. Using the same sample, have a student model how to sit facing you while giving feedback on the sample for 30 uninterrupted seconds.

Support That Statement *(cont.)*

Apply/Analyze

7. Divide students into pairs. Have students face their partners while seated at their desks. Assign one student in each pair as Partner *A* and one to be Partner *B*.

8. Have both partners read the writing sample from his or her partner, paying particular attention to the use of thesis and supporting statements.

9. Have Partner *A* begin by sharing his or her thinking with Partner *B,* while Partner *B* only listens for 30 seconds. After 30 seconds, Partner *B* responds to Partner *A*.

10. Have students switch roles, so Partner *B* shares while Partner *A* listens. Then, Partner *A* provides insights or responds to the feedback.

11. Distribute the *Feedback Sheet* (page 108) to students. Students should then take a few minutes to record on their activity sheets what their partners say for further consideration and use that to revise and further develop their writing.

Evaluate/Create

12. Allow students time to revise and edit their writing to include clear thesis statements and relevant supporting evidence.

13. Provide students with writing previously submitted or written in class. Ask students to review the work and evaluate the thesis statement and support, given their new learning. Allow students to revise and rewrite previous work to strengthen the connection between the thesis statement and support.

Name: _____   Date: _____

Feedback Sheet

Directions: Record the feedback given to you by your partner.

1. What did your partner feel were the strengths of your writing? Be specific.

_____

_____

_____

2. According to your partner, where and how did you effectively use a thesis and supporting statements?

_____

_____

_____

3. Where did your partner feel you could improve your writing? Why?

_____

_____

_____

4. According to your partner, where and how could you strengthen your use of a thesis and supporting statements?

_____

_____

_____

Origin of Our Rights

Brain-Powered Strategy	**Standard**
Just Say It	Understands that the Constitution is a written document which states that the fundamental purposes of American government are to protect individual rights and promote the common good

Vocabulary Words

- common good
- constitutional rights
- fundamental purpose
- individual rights

Materials

- *Constitutional Rights Cards* (pages 111–114)
- *Feedback Sheet* (page 115)
- constitutional rights resources (e.g., Internet, textbook)
- chart paper

Preparation Note: Prior to the lesson, cut apart the *Constitutional Rights Cards* (pages 111–114).

Procedures

Model

1. Review the idea of constitutional rights and their origins.

2. Read students a sample constitutional right, and demonstrate how to discuss or hypothesize its origins. Ask a volunteer to be your partner, and give "feedback" on the origin, following the same structure as the *Feedback Sheet* activity sheet (page 115).

3. As a class, discuss the feedback, noting the importance of hearing the feedback as a way to understand different ways of thinking while discussing history.

4. Tell students that they will be doing a strategy called *Just Say It*. (For detailed information on this strategy, see page 16.)

5. Divide students into pairs. Using a different sample, have a student model how to sit facing you while giving feedback on the sample for 30 uninterrupted seconds.

Origin of Our Rights *(cont.)*

Apply/Analyze

6. Have students face their partners while seated at their desks. Assign one student in each pair as Partner *A* and one to be Partner *B*.

7. Give each set of partners a *Constitutional Rights Card* to discuss and hypothesize its origins.

8. Have Partner *A* begin by sharing his or her thinking with Partner *B,* while Partner *B* only listens for 30 seconds. After 30 seconds, Partner *B* responds to Partner *A*.

9. Have students switch roles, so Partner *B* shares while Partner *A* listens. Then, Partner *A* provides insights or responds to the feedback.

10. Distribute the *Feedback Sheet* activity sheet to students. Students should then take a few minutes to record their partners' thoughts and insights using the activity sheet.

Evaluate/Create

11. Using the assigned constitutional right, have students use materials and resources, such as their text or the Internet, to research the origin of their constitutional right. Then, have student pairs create a chart on a sheet of chart paper comparing and contrasting the origin of two or more constitutional rights.

12. Have students work together to create a bulletin board or poster to illustrate the origin of the constitutional right.

Constitutional Rights Cards

Teacher Directions: Cut apart the cards below.

Constitutional Rights Cards *(cont.)*

Constitutional Rights Cards *(cont.)*

to enjoy privacy

to exclude others from private residences

to petition for redress of grievances

to due process of law

Constitutional Rights Cards (cont.)

not to testify against oneself

to have a speedy and public trial

to have an impartial jury of peers

to vote in elections

Name: _____   Date: _____

Feedback Sheet

· ·

Directions: Record the feedback given to you by your partner.

1. What did your partner feel were the strengths of your thinking?

    _____

    _____

    _____

    _____

2. According to your partner, where and how did you effectively think about the meaning of the constitutional right and its origin?

    _____

    _____

    _____

    _____

3. Where did your partner feel you could improve your reasoning?

    _____

    _____

    _____

4. According to your partner, where and how could you strengthen your reasoning about the meaning of the constitutional right and its origin?

    _____

    _____

    _____

Evidence to Support Point of View

Brain-Powered Strategy	Standard
Just Say It	Describe how a narrator's or speaker's point of view influences how events are described

Vocabulary Words	**Materials**
• first person • narrator • omniscient • point of view • third person	• *Feedback Sheet* (page 118) • chart paper • variety of stories and passages demonstrating point of view

Procedures

Model

1. Discuss point of view with students. As a class, brainstorm a list of different points of view on the board or on a sheet of chart paper and discuss how you might recognize each when reading.

2. Discuss how the speaker's or narrator's point of view can influence your interpretation of the text and how events are described.

3. Explain that today you will focus on giving a partner helpful feedback about reading critically. Tell students that they will each read passages and discuss how the narrator's point of view influences the text.

4. Tell students that they will be doing a strategy called *Just Say It*. (For detailed information on this strategy, see page 16.)

5. Read a sample text aloud and demonstrate how to speak about the text and how point of view influences your interpretation of the text and how events are described. Ask students to give you feedback, following the same structure as the *Feedback Sheet* activity sheet (page 118).

6. Discuss the feedback, noting the importance of hearing the feedback as a way to improve your critical-reading skills.

7. Using the same sample, have a student model how to sit facing you while giving feedback on the sample for 30 uninterrupted seconds.

Evidence to Support
Point of View *(cont.)*

Apply/Analyze

8. Divide students into pairs. Have students face their partners while seated at their desks. Assign one student in each pair as Partner *A* and one to be Partner *B*.

9. Distribute the stories, reading passages, and the *Feedback Sheet* activity sheet to students. Have both partners read the reading passage, paying particular attention to how the narrator's point of view influences the text and your interpretation.

10. Have Partner *A* begin by sharing his or her thinking with Partner *B,* while Partner *B* only listens for 30 seconds. After 30 seconds, Partner *B* responds to Partner *A*.

11. Have students switch roles, so Partner *B* shares while Partner *A* listens. Then, Partner *A* provides insights or responds to the feedback.

12. Students should then take a few minutes to record, what their partners say on the *Feedback Sheet* activity sheet for further consideration.

Evaluate/Create

13. Instruct students to work with partners to create a diagram, noting how a different point of view may have influenced how events were described.

14. Have students rewrite portions of the passage in a different point of view.

15. Ask students to write three statements generalizing the use of point of view.

16. Provide each student with two texts demonstrating different points of view. Have students evaluate the accuracy and completeness of the information from each point of view.

Name: _____ Date: _____

Feedback Sheet

Directions: Record the feedback given to you by your partner.

1. What did your partner feel were the strengths of your writing?

_____

_____

_____

2. According to your partner, where and how did you effectively use dialogue and description to develop experiences and events?

_____

_____

_____

3. Where did your partner feel you could improve your writing to get your point of view across?

_____

_____

_____

4. According to your partner, where and how could you strengthen your use of dialogue and description to develop experiences and events?

_____

_____

Parts of Speech

Brain-Powered Strategy	**Standard**
Reverse, Reverse!	Explain the function of conjunctions, prepositions, and interjections in general and their function in particular sentences

Vocabulary Words	**Materials**
• conjunction	• *Parts of Speech Cards* (pages 121–126)
• interjection	• timer or clock
• preposition	• index cards
	• writing paper

Preparation Note: Prior to the lesson, cut apart the *Parts of Speech Cards* (pages 121–126) so each group has one card.

Procedures

Model

1. Review the functions of conjunctions, prepositions, and interjections in general and their function in particular sentences with students.

2. Tell students that they will be doing a strategy called *Reverse, Reverse!* (For detailed information on this strategy, see page 17.)

3. Select five volunteers and have them sit or stand in a circle. State a conjunction, preposition, or interjection. Ask the first person to state the part of speech and the second person to state its general function.

4. Going clockwise, ask the next student to quickly state another word demonstrating that part of speech. Explain to students that they are to state their answers quickly, within five seconds. If they do not, or if they state an incorrect response, then the direction of participation reverses.

5. Repeat Steps 3–4 with a new part of speech but this time model the role of judge, making sure that the answers are correct and participation meets time guidelines. The judge can also halt the flow to ask a student to justify the response he or she has just given.

Parts of Speech *(cont.)*

Apply/Analyze

6. Divide students into groups of six or seven. Have them sit or stand in a circle. Appoint a student to act as judge for each circle.

7. Provide each judge with a set of the *Parts of Speech Cards*.

8. Have the judge read a card. Do the strategy as practiced.

9. Continue until a predetermined amount of time or a certain number of times around the circle has been met.

Evaluate/Create

10. Distribute an index card to each student. Using the cards, have students create their own set of parts of speech cards, making sure to write the answer and function of each part of speech on the back of the card.

11. Distribute writing paper to students. Ask students to write sentences or paragraphs demonstrating they understand and know how to use the parts of speech.

12. Have students switch sentences or paragraphs with a partner and determine if the parts of speech are used correctly or if there is a better choice.

13. Provide each student with a single conjunction, preposition, or interjection. Have them create a review for the part of speech, defending and supporting its use in writing.

Parts of Speech Cards

Teacher Directions: Cut apart the cards below.

so	for
not	yet

Parts of Speech Cards *(cont.)*

and	**but**
or	**nor**

Parts of Speech Cards *(cont.)*

above

behind

below

beside

Parts of Speech Cards (cont.)

on

by

near

from

Parts of Speech Cards *(cont.)*

wow

oh my

ahem

cheers

Parts of Speech Cards *(cont.)*

woo-hoo

shhh

that's great

sorry

Amending the Constitution

Brain-Powered Strategy	Standard
Reverse, Reverse!	Knows that the government was created by people who had the following beliefs: the government is established by and for the people, the people have the right to choose their representatives, and the people have the right to change their government and the Constitution

Vocabulary Words

- authority
- constitutional
- convention
- majority vote
- propose
- ratification

Materials

- timer or clock
- index cards
- multiple texts about the amendment process

Procedures

Model

1. Review with students the idea that people have the right to change their government and the Constitution. Also, review how a bill becomes a law.

2. Tell students that they will be doing a strategy called *Reverse, Reverse!* (For detailed information on this strategy, see page 17.)

3. Select five volunteers, and have them sit or stand in a circle. Demonstrate the strategy with the chronological order of how to tie shoes. State the first step, *tighten the laces.*

4. Going clockwise, ask the next student to quickly state the next step in tying a pair of shoes. Explain to students that they are to state their answers quickly, within about five seconds. If they do not, or if they state an incorrect response, then the direction of participation reverses.

5. Repeat Steps 3–4 with a new example, such as walking to the office from your classroom, but this time model the role of judge, making sure that the answers are correct and participation meets time guidelines. The judge can also halt the flow to ask a student to justify the response he or she has just given.

Amending the Constitution *(cont.)*

Apply/Analyze

6. Divide students into groups of six or seven and have them sit or stand in a circle. Appoint a student to act as judge for each circle.

7. Ask each judge to state the first step in how a bill becomes a law.

8. Continue until a predetermined amount of time or number of times around the circle has been met.

Evaluate/Create

9. Distribute an index card to each student. Using the cards, ask students to create their own flow charts illustrating the process of how a bill becomes a law.

10. Have students switch flow charts and evaluate the relevancy, accuracy, and completeness of information.

11. Ask students to compare and contrast the process of how a bill becomes a law with the process of creating a bill.

12. Provide students with multiple texts about the process of how a bill becomes a law. Ask students to evaluate the authors' purpose, main idea, and perspectives between and among texts.

That's the Order

Brain-Powered Strategy	Standard
Reverse, Reverse!	Explain how a series of chapters, scenes, or stanzas fits together to provide the overall structure of a particular story, drama, or poem

Vocabulary Words

- chapter
- scene
- stanza
- structure of story, drama, poem

Materials

- short passages or poems demonstrating structure or chronological order
- timer or clock

Preparation Note: Prior to the lesson, choose a number of short passages or poems demonstrating structure or chronological order.

Procedures

Model

1. Model a reading passage in a narrative or informational text where students can cite details or examples.

2. Tell students that they will be doing a strategy called *Reverse, Reverse!* (For detailed information on this strategy, see page 17.)

3. Select five student volunteers and have them sit or stand in a circle. State an event in the story, drama, or poem.

4. Going clockwise, ask the next student to quickly state the next event in chronological order. Explain to students that they are to state their answers quickly, within five seconds. If they do not, or if they state an incorrect response, then the direction of participation reverses.

5. Repeat Steps 3–4 with a new event or passage, but this time model the role of judge, making sure that the facts are correct and participation meets time guidelines. The judge can also halt the flow to ask a student to justify the response he or she has just given.

That's the Order *(cont.)*

Apply/Analyze

6. Divide students into groups of six or seven. Have them sit or stand in a circle. Appoint a student to act as judge for each circle.

7. Provide each judge with a set of passages.

8. Have the judge read the passages or poems. Do the strategy as practiced.

9. Continue until a predetermined amount of time or number of times around the circle has been met.

Evaluate/Create

10. Ask students to think about familiar texts they have read in the course or during the year. Have them create a key a judge may use during *Reverse, Reverse!* to check student understanding. Play *Reverse, Reverse!* again if time allows.

11. Provide students with a nonfiction text and a fiction text demonstrating chronological order. Ask students to evaluate the structure and text features, such as chronological order, that help readers quickly and accurately receive information in each.

Convert It

Brain-Powered Strategy	**Standard**
WPH Accordion	Convert among different-sized standard measurement units within a given measurement system and use these conversions in solving multi-step, real world problems

Vocabulary Words

- convert
- metric system
- United States customary system

Materials

- *Convert It Cards* (pages 133–136)
- envelopes
- half sheets of paper (cut horizontally)
- colored pencils or crayons
- various informational texts using measurements

Preparation Note: Prior to the lesson, cut apart the *Convert It Cards* (pages 133–136). Place one part of the cards in envelopes to be hidden from students.

Procedures

Model

1. Introduce the lesson with the story/myth of how the measurement of a foot doesn't mean any foot, but was the length of Hercules' foot. Discuss the importance of uniform measurements that can be converted so they are practical and easy to use. Explain that there are now two common measurement systems in the world, metric and United States customary. Discuss in more detail the one that you will be converting with.

2. Tell students that they will be doing a strategy called *WPH Accordion.* (For detailed information on this strategy, see page 18.)

3. Draw a three-column chart on the board. Put a *W* in the first column, a *P* in the next column, and an *H* in the last column. Create illustrations to remind students what each column represents, such as a face for the *W* column, an arrow pointing to the right (future) for the *P*, and three horizontal lines by the *H* for a list of what happened.

4. Begin reading a unit conversion math problem that you will be solving today, or use one from the *Convert It Cards.* **Note:** Read the problem aloud only; do not provide students with their own copy so that you can control the timing of the information they will receive. Think aloud, saying, "The word _____ (e.g., inch, yard, mile, centimeter, meter) in the problem tells me that this is about _____ (name the system of measurement). This means that I will need to convert using this system."

Convert It (cont.)

5. Write the name of the unit in the *W* column. For the *P* column, think aloud so students get a feel for what other units of measurement you might convert to. For example, if the problem you are reading uses yards, you might convert to inches, feet, or miles. Ask students to record their predictions in the *P* column along with an equation for each conversion. For example: 12 inches = 1 foot. Finish reading the problem and record the actual unit of measurement you need to convert to, along with the equation specific to the problem.

Apply/Analyze

6. Divide students into groups of three. Distribute a half sheet of paper to each student, along with a picture card and an envelope containing the picture card's counterpart from the *Convert It Cards* to each group.

7. Ask students to fold the paper in half and then in half again to create four sections. Have students bend the first crease back, second crease forward, and so on, in order to create an accordion effect.

8. Instruct students to turn the closed paper so that the first fold is at the top. While keeping the paper closed to the other sections, have students write down the name of the measurement system in the front section.

9. On the second section, have students label a *W* in a corner for *who* or *what* is involved and draw a face. On the third section, have students label the corner *P* for *predict*, and draw an arrow pointing to the right, indicating the future.

10. For the last section, instruct students to label an *H* in the corner, and draw three short horizontal parallel lines to list what *happens*.

11. In their groups, have students read the phrase on the picture card to determine who or what is involved. Record the information on the *W* section. Have students record their own thoughts in the *P* section for what they might convert to and the corresponding equation. Share group members' predictions.

12. Prompt students to read the cards in the envelopes to discover what happens, and then record their findings and the equation specific to the problem in the *H* section.

13. Jigsaw students so that there is at least one representative for each problem in each group. Have students share what they learned about the problem.

Evaluate/Create

14. To debrief, ask students to discuss the following questions. Guide them, as needed, to see patterns in conversions:

- Were your predictions on target?

- Is it all right to have a wrong prediction?

- What clues or prior knowledge led you to predict accurately?

- How did your thinking change?

- How does thinking about the conversion before you do it help you when you are problem solving?

15. Either independently or in pairs, have students create a conversion problem for another group to solve using the *WPH Accordion* strategy.

16. Provide students with informational texts using measurements. Have students categorize and evaluate the units of measurement in each. For example, students might say scientific texts use the metric system.

Convert It Cards

Teacher Directions: Cut apart the cards below.

Tyler played basketball for 4 hours …

… how many minutes did he play?

Jose has 1 gallon of juice …

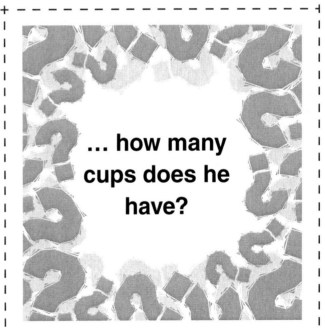

… how many cups does he have?

Convert It Cards *(cont.)*

Paula spun a toy hoop for 2 minutes …

… how many seconds did she spin a toy hoop?

Ethan jumped 4 feet …

… how many inches did he jump?

Convert It Cards *(cont.)*

Bobby baked his bread for $1\frac{1}{2}$ hours ...

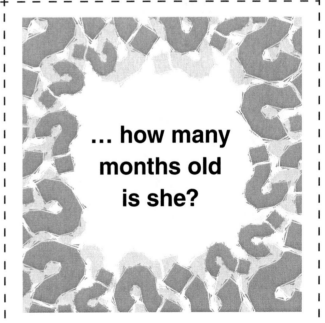

... how many minutes did he bake it?

Jacqueline is two years old ...

... how many months old is she?

Convert It Cards *(cont.)*

Isa needs 72 inches of string …

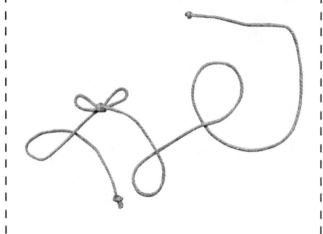

… how many
centimeters
does she
need?

Eva has 24 inches left to decorate on her poster …

… how many
feet did she
have left
to decorate?

Food Chain Accordion

Brain-Powered Strategy	Standard
WPH Accordion	Knows the organization of simple food chains and food webs

Vocabulary Words	Materials
• carnivore • food chain • herbivore • omnivore • photosynthetic plants	• *Food Chain Cards* (page 139) • envelopes • half sheets of paper (cut horizontally) • colored pencils or crayons • informational texts about food chains in a variety of biomes

Preparation Note: Prior to the lesson, write the consumers of the food chain you are studying along with the foods they consume on the *Food Chain Cards* (page 139). Then, cut the cards apart. Place the cards' counterparts in envelopes.

Procedures

Model

1. Introduce the lesson by discussing or reviewing the ecosystem you are studying. Explain the idea that the parts of the food chain are innerconnected and depend upon each other for survival.

2. Tell students that they will be doing a strategy called *WPH Accordion.* (For detailed information on this strategy, see page 18.)

3. Draw a three-column chart on the board. Put a *W* in the first column, a *P* in the next column, and an *H* in the last column. Create illustrations to remind students what each column represents, such as a face for the *W* column, an arrow pointing to the right (future) for the *P*, and three horizontal lines by the *H* for a list of what happened.

4. Complete an example food chain accordion together. Begin by stating the name of a consumer. Think aloud, saying, "I know that the _____ (*consumer*) lives in this ecosystem and that it eats other things in this ecosystem. I am going to model for you how to complete a food chain accordion."

5. Write the name of the consumer in the *W* column. For the *P* column, think aloud while creating a list of what it eats. For example, if the consumer is a *cheetah,* you can name *guinea fowl, gazelle,* and *deer.* Ask students to record their predictions in the *P* column.

Food Chain Accordion *(cont.)*

Apply/Analyze

6. Divide students into groups, no more than three per group. Distribute a half sheet of paper to each student, along with an envelope containing one theme *Food Chain Card* and its counterpart.

7. Instruct students to fold the paper in half and then in half again to create four equal sections. Then, have students bend the first crease back, second crease forward, and so on, in order to create an accordion effect.

8. Instruct students to turn the closed paper so that the first fold is at the top. While keeping the paper closed to the other sections, have students write down the name of the ecosystem in the front section with colored pencils or crayons.

9. On the second section, have students label a *W* in a corner for *who* or *what* is involved and draw a face. On the third section, have students label the corner *P* for *predict,* and draw an arrow pointing to the right, indicating the future.

10. For the last section, instruct students to label an *H* in the corner, and draw three short horizontal parallel lines to list what *happens*.

11. In their groups, have students read the consumer from the *Food Chain Card* and record the information in the *W* section. Have students record their own predictions in the *P* section for what it might eat. Share group members' predictions and record all thoughts.

12. Prompt students to read the card in the envelope and record what it actually eats in the *H* section.

13. Jigsaw students so that there is at least one representative for each consumer in each group. Have students share what they learned about each.

Evaluate/Create

14. To debrief, ask students to discuss the following questions. Guide them, as needed, to see patterns:

- Were your predictions on target?

- Is it all right to have a wrong prediction?

- Did your predictions make sense?

- What clues or prior knowledge led you to predict accurately?

- What clues did you miss that would have helped you with a more accurate prediction?

- How did your thinking change?

- How did prior knowledge help you with learning new knowledge?

15. Either independently or in pairs, have students compare and contrast the information about their WPH charts. Have students write a short informational paragraph where they synthesize the information about the two consumers and draw conclusions about their roles in the food chain.

16. Provide students with informational texts about food chains in a variety of different biomes. Have students analyze and evaluate the information, drawing conclusions about the information presented in multiple texts.

Food Chain Cards

Teacher Directions: Copy as many cards as needed. For each card, write the name of a consumer on the left and what it eats on the right. Then, cut the cards apart.

Shades of Meaning Accordion

Brain-Powered Strategy	Standard
WPH Accordion	Demonstrate understanding of figurative language, word relationships, and nuances in word meanings

Vocabulary Words	Materials
• figurative language • nuances in word meanings • word relationships	• book or short passages of a text • chart paper • half sheet of paper (cut horizontally) • colored pencils or crayons • dictionaries (*optional*) • writing paper • informational texts demonstrating shades of meaning

Preparation Note: Prior to the lesson, identify figurative language or words from the selected passages or book demonstrating shades of meaning.

Procedures

Model

1. Introduce the lesson by writing the following sentence on the board or on a sheet of chart paper: *I am tired*. Discuss the meaning of the word *tired*. Brainstorm a list of words that are more powerful (stronger) in meaning than *tired,* and discuss words that are weaker (less strong) than *tired*. Explain that today you will look critically at your reading and make predictions about shades of meaning.

2. Tell students that they will be doing a strategy called *WPH Accordion*. (For detailed information on this strategy, see page 18.)

3. Draw a three-column chart on the board. Put a *W* in the first column, a *P* in the next column, and an *H* in the last column. Create illustrations to remind students what each column represents, such as a face for the *W* column, an arrow pointing to the right (future) for the *P*, and three horizontal lines by the *H* for a list of what happened.

4. Complete an example "Shades of Meaning" accordion together. Begin by reading a paragraph or short passage from the selected text. Think aloud, saying, "I know that the word _____ can mean a variety of things. I am going to model for you how to complete a 'Shades of Meaning' accordion."

Shades of Meaning Accordion *(cont.)*

5. Write the selected word in the *W* column. For the *P* column, think aloud while writing. Say, "I think a word that is weaker is _____ because it means _____. On the other hand, I think a stronger word would be _____. I am using context clues from the passage to help me figure out exactly what the author means by this word." For example, if the sample word is *hungry,* you might say a weaker word is *peckish* and a stronger word is *famished.*

6. Tell students that if you continue reading, they would continue to gather clues to the meaning of the word, but you are not ready to do that (leave a cliff-hanger).

Apply/Analyze

7. Divide students into groups of three. Distribute a half sheet of paper and a word or phrase from the text to each student.

8. Ask students to fold the paper in half and then in half again to create four equal sections. Have students bend the first crease back, second crease forward, and so on, in order to create an accordion effect.

9. Instruct students to turn the closed paper so that the first fold is at the top. While keeping the paper closed to the other sections, have students write down the name of the text in the front section.

10. On the second section, have students label a *W* in a corner for *who* or *what* is involved and draw a face. On the third section, have students label the corner *P* for *predict*, and draw an arrow pointing to the right, indicating the future.

11. For the last section, instruct students to label an *H* in the corner, and draw three short horizontal parallel lines to list what *happens.*

12. In their groups, have students read the passages of the text that contain the word they are studying. Record the information in the *W* section. Have students record their own predictions in the *P* section for what words would be weaker and stronger in meaning. Have groups share.

13. Prompt students to read on and record what it actually means from the text and/or dictionaries in the *H* section.

14. Jigsaw students so that there is at least one representative for each word in a group. Have students share what they learned about each word and its use.

Evaluate/Create

15. Ask students to discuss the questions below. Guide them to see patterns that will help them when reading other texts:

- Were your predictions on target?

- Is it all right to have a wrong prediction?

- What clues or prior knowledge led you to predict accurately?

- How did your thinking change?

16. In pairs, have students compare and contrast the information about their WPH charts. Distribute writing paper to students, and have them write a short informational paragraph where they synthesize the information about the nuances of word meaning.

17. Provide students with a variety of texts demonstrating nuances in word meaning. For example, provide students with a variety of texts that demonstrate different ways of using the word *said* such as *yelled*, *asked*, *whispered*, etc. Have students construct a flow chart categorizing the words according to shades of meaning.

Replacing with Equivalent Fractions

Brain-Powered Strategy	Standard
That's a Wrap!	Add and subtract fractions with unlike denominators by replacing given fractions with equivalent fractions in such a way as to produce an equivalent sum or difference of fractions with like denominators

Vocabulary Words	Materials
• denominators • difference • equivalent • mixed numbers • sum	• index cards • hole punch • yarn or metal ring • writing paper • interview props (*optional*)

Procedures

Model

1. After students have learned about how to replace fractions with equivalent fractions in order to make like denominators for adding and subtracting, access students' background knowledge by asking them, "What steps do you follow when you are adding or subtracting fractions with unlike denominators?"

2. Allow students time to share their answers with the class. Record student responses on the board.

3. Transition to the lesson by asking students about their study habits. Explain that a lot of times, we think we know something because it looks familiar, but we do not *really* know it.

4. Tell students that they will be doing a strategy called *That's a Wrap!* (For detailed information on this strategy, see page 19.)

5. Say, "Today, we will learn one way to study by practicing how to take important information and turn it into a question. Think back on all that we have learned about replacing given fractions with equivalent fractions in such a way as to produce an equivalent sum or difference of fractions with like denominators." Record the key vocabulary, steps, and other key information they remember.

6. Help students rank the importance of each. Choose a few of the parts and turn them into questions and answers that are written in complete sentences. For example, students may come up with questions such as *What makes having like denominators easier to add and subtract fractions?*

Replacing with Equivalent Fractions *(cont.)*

Apply/Analyze

7. Distribute about 10 index cards to each student. Using the study guide, notes, handouts, charts, or other resources, have students practice writing the key information in the form of questions and answers. Tell students to write their questions on the fronts of the cards and their answers on the backs of the cards. Then, use a hole punch to join the cards with yarn or a metal ring. Tell students they will use these questions later to write a script for a mock interview.

Evaluate/Create

8. Once students have recorded some questions, ask them to confirm with their neighbors why the questions are important, and justify why they "really need to know" the answers. Model how to determine importance, if necessary.

9. Divide students into groups of four or five. Using the questions they identified as "really need to know," have students work in their groups to write a script as if they were giving an interview.

10. Have students determine their roles. They can choose famous people, be someone in the school, or make up names that relate to the matter, such as Mr. Factor, Mrs. Denominator, or Ms. Equivalent. Students can ask one another questions for practice.

11. Students may create props to make the interviews even greater successes. Allow them to dress up or use fake microphones for the interviews.

12. Allow each group an opportunity to be interviewed by those in the audience. The audience should ask questions they heard from the presenters' scripts. Encourage presenters not to look at their scripts for the answers, so that they begin to understand the difference between "know" and "still need to learn." If students do not know an answer, teach them to say, "That's a great question! Let me find out," and have them write the question. At the end of each interview, have students say, "That's a Wrap!"

13. Either in pairs or small groups, have students create a statement on writing paper that synthesizes their understanding of equivalent fractions and their role in solving problems. Then, have student groups share their statements with the class.

Let's Study Water Forms

Brain-Powered Strategy	**Standard**
That's a Wrap!	Knows that matter has different states and that each state has distinct physical properties; some common materials such as water can be changed from one state to another by heating or cooling

Vocabulary Words

- gas
- liquid
- physical properties
- solid
- states of matter

Materials

- text passages about the states of matter
- index cards
- hole punch
- yarn or metal ring
- interview props (*optional*)
- drawing paper

Preparation Note: Prior to the lesson, collect text passages about the states of matter.

Procedures

Model

1. After students have learned about the states of matter, access students' background knowledge by asking them, "What are the distinct physical properties of each state of matter?"

2. Allow students time to share their answers with the class. Record student responses on the board.

3. Transition to the lesson by asking students about their study habits. Explain that a lot of times, we think we know something because it looks familiar, but we do not *really* know it.

4. Tell students that they will be doing a strategy called *That's a Wrap!* (For detailed information on this strategy, see page 19.)

5. Say, "Today we will learn one way to study by practicing how to take important information and turn it into a question. Think back on all that we have learned about the states of matter and how it can change states." Record the key vocabulary, steps, and other key information they remember.

6. Help students rank the importance of each. Choose a few of the parts and turn them into questions and answers that are written in complete sentences. For example, students may ask questions such as *How can you tell the physical properties of matter?*

Let's Study Water Forms *(cont.)*

Apply/Analyze

7. Distribute about 10 index cards to each student. Using the study guide, notes, handouts, charts, or other resources, have students practice writing the key information in the form of questions and answers. Tell students to write their questions on the fronts of the cards and their answers on the backs of the cards. Then, use a hole punch to join the cards with yarn or a metal ring. Tell students they will use these questions later to write a script for a mock interview.

Evaluate/Create

8. Once students have recorded some questions, ask them to confirm with a partner why the questions are important and justify why they "really need to know" the answers. Model how to determine importance, if necessary.

9. Divide students into groups of four or five. Using the questions they identified as "really need to know," have students work in their groups to write a script as if they were giving an interview.

10. Have students determine their roles. They can choose famous people, be someone in the school, or make up names that relate to the matter, such as Mr. Gas, Mrs. Solid, or Ms. Liquid. Students can ask one another questions for practice.

11. Students may create props to make the interviews even greater successes. Allow them to dress up or use fake microphones for the interviews.

12. Allow each group an opportunity to be interviewed by those in the audience. The audience should ask questions they heard from the presenters' script. Encourage presenters not to look at their scripts for the answers, so that they begin to understand the difference between "know" and "still need to learn." If students do not know an answer, teach them to say, "That's a great question! Let me find out," and have them write the question. At the end of each interview, have students say, "That's a Wrap!"

13. Provide each student with an informational text about the stages of matter to read independently. As a whole class, discuss the similarities and differences between the texts. Analyze and evaluate how each text describes and explains the stages, depending upon the author's purpose.

14. Either in pairs or small groups, have students create a flow chart on a sheet of drawing paper that synthesizes their understanding of the states of matter.

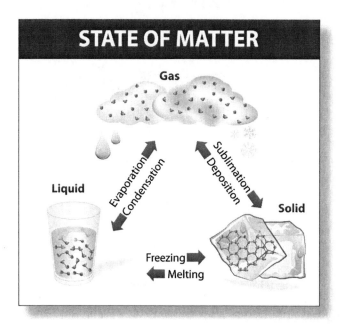

Let's Study Figurative Language

Brain-Powered Strategy	Standard
That's a Wrap!	Interpret figurative language, including similes and metaphors, in context

Vocabulary Words

- figurative language
- in context
- metaphors
- similes

Materials

- reading passages demonstrating the use of figurative language
- index cards
- hole punch
- yarn or metal ring
- writing paper
- interview props (*optional*)

Preparation Note: Prior to the lesson, collect reading passages demonstrating the use of figurative language.

Procedures

Model

1. After students have learned about how to interpret figurative language in context, access students' background knowledge by asking them, "What steps do you follow when you are trying to determine the meaning of figurative language?"

2. Allow students time to share their answers with the class. Record student responses on the board.

3. Transition to the lesson by asking students about their study habits. Explain that a lot of times, we think we know something because it looks familiar, but we do not *really* know it.

4. Tell students that they will be doing a strategy called *That's a Wrap!* (For detailed information on this strategy, see page 19.)

5. Say, "Today we will learn one way to study by practicing how to take important information and turn it into a question. Think back on all that we have learned about interpreting figurative language." Record the key vocabulary, steps, and other key information they remember.

6. Help students rank the importance of each. Choose a few of the parts and turn them into questions and answers that are written in complete sentences. For example, students may ask questions such as *What key words will help me distinguish which type of figurative language is being used?*

Let's Study Figurative Language *(cont.)*

Apply/Analyze

7. Distribute about 10 index cards to each student. Using the study guide, notes, handouts, charts, or other resources, have students practice writing the key information in the form of questions and answers. Tell students to write their questions on the fronts of the cards and their answers on the backs of the cards. Then, use a hole punch to join the cards with yarn or a metal ring. Tell students they will use these questions later to write a script for a mock interview.

Evaluate/Create

8. Once students have recorded some questions, ask them to confirm with a partner why the questions are important and justify why they "really need to know" the answers. Model how to determine importance, if necessary.

9. Divide students into groups of four or five. Using the questions they identified as "really need to know," have students work in their groups to write a script as if they were giving an interview.

10. Have students determine their roles. They can choose famous people, be someone in the school, or make up names that relate to the matter, such as Mr. Simile, Mrs. Meta Phor, or Ms. Figurative. Students can ask each other questions for practice.

11. Students may create props to make the interviews even greater successes. Allow them to dress up or use fake microphones for the interview.

12. Allow each group an opportunity to be interviewed by those in the audience. The audience should ask questions they heard from the presenters' script. Encourage presenters not to look at their scripts for the answers, so that they begin to understand the difference between "know" and "still need to learn." If students do not know an answer, teach them to say, "That's a great question! Let me find out," and have them write the question. At the end of each interview, have students say, "That's a Wrap!"

13. Either in pairs or small groups, have students create a statement that synthesizes their understanding of the role of figurative language. Then, have student groups share their statements with the class.

14. Provide each student with a text demonstrating the use of figurative language. As a whole class, discuss the similarities and differences between the texts. Analyze and evaluate how each text uses figurative language.

References Cited

Ainsworth, Larry. 2003. *Unwrapping the Standards: A Simple Process to Make Standards Manageable.* Englewood, CO: Lead+Learn Press.

Anderson, Lorin and David Krathwohl (Eds.). 2001. *Taxonomy for Learning, Teaching, and Assessing: A Revision of Bloom's Taxonomy of Educational Objectives.* Boston, MA: Pearson Education Group.

Baker, Linda. 2009. "Historical Roots of Inquiry in Metacognition." Retrieved from http://www.education.com/reference/article/metacognition.

Bloom, Benjamin (Ed.). 1956. *Taxonomy of Educational Objectives.* New York: David McKay Company.

Covington, Martin V. 2000. "Goal Theory, Motivation, and School Achievement: An Integrative Review." Retrieved from http://www2.csdm.qc.ca/SaintEmile/bernet/annexes/ASS6826/Covington2000.pdf.

Csikszentmihalyi, Mihaly. 1996. *Creativity: Flow and the Psychology of Discovery and Invention.* New York: HarperCollins.

Doidge, Norman. 2007. *The Brain That Changes Itself: Stories of Personal Triumph from the Frontiers of Brain Science.* New York, NY: Penguin Books.

Flavell, John H. 1979. "Metacognition and Cognitive Monitoring: A New Area of Cognitive-Developmental Inquiry." *American Psychologist* 34: 906–911.

Harris, Bryan, and Cassandra Goldberg. 2012. *75 Quick and Easy Solutions to Common Classroom Disruptions.* Florence, KY: Routledge.

Huntington's Outreach Program for Education, at Stanford (HOPES). 2010. "Neuroplasticity." http://www.stanford.edu/group/hopes/cgi-bin/wordpress/2010/06/neuroplasticity.

Immordino-Yang, Mary H. and Matthias Faeth. 2010. "The Role of Emotion and Skilled Intuition in Learning." In *Mind, Brain, and Education: Neuroscience Implications for the Classroom*, edited by David A. Sousa, 69–83. Bloomington, IN: Solution Tree.

Jensen, Eric. 2005. *Teaching with the Brain in Mind.* Alexandria, VA: Association for Supervision and Curriculum Development.

McCombs, Barbara L. 1997. "Understanding the Keys to Motivation to Learn." Retrieved from http://incolor.inetnebr.com/fadams/motivation_exercise.htm.

Medina, J. 2008. *Brain Rules: 12 Principles for Surviving and Thriving at Work, Home, and School.* Seattle, WA: Pear Press.

Merzenich, Dr. Michael. 2013. *Soft-Wired: How the New Science of Brain Plasticity Can Change Your Life.* San Francisco, CA: Parnassus Publishing, LLC.

Overbaugh, Richard C. and Lynn Schultz. n.d. *Bloom's Taxonomy.* Retrieved from http://www.odu.edu/educ/roverbau/Bloom/blooms_taxonomy.htm.

References Cited *(cont.)*

Ratey, John J. 2008. *Spark: The Revolutionary New Science of Exercise and the Brain.* New York, NY: Little, Brown and Company.

Rock, David. 2009. *Your Brain at Work: Strategies for Overcoming Distraction, Regaining Focus, and Working Smarter All Day Long.* New York: HarperCollins.

Roth, LaVonna. 2012. *Brain-Powered Strategies to Engage All Learners.* Huntington Beach, CA: Shell Education.

Sousa, David A. 2006. *How the Brain Learns*, 3rd ed. Bloomington, IN: Solution Tree.

Thomas, Alice and Glenda Thorne. 2009. "How to Increase Higher Order Thinking." Retrieved from http://www.cdl.org/resourcelibrary/articles/HOT.php?type=subject&id=18.

Van Tassell, Gene. 2004. "Neural Pathway Development." Retrieved from http://www.brains.org/path.htm.

Vaynman, Shoshanna, Zhe Ying, and Fernando Gomez-Pinilla. 2004. "Hippocampal BDNF Mediates the Efficacy of Exercise on Synaptic Plasticity and Cognition." *European Journal of Neuroscience* 20: 2580–2590.

Webb, Norman L. 2005. "Alignment, Depth of Knowledge, and Change." Presented at the 50th annual meeting of the Florida Educational Research Association, Miami, FL. Abstract retrieved from http://facstaff.wcer.wisc.edu/normw/MIAMI%20FLORIDA%20FINAL%20 slides%2011-15-05.pdf.

Wiggins, Grant and Jay McTighe. 2005. *Understanding by Design*, 2nd ed. Upper Saddle River, NJ: Prentice Hall.

Willis, Judy. 2006. *Research-Based Strategies to Ignite Student Learning.* Alexandria, VA: Association for Supervision and Curriculum Development (ASCD).

———. 2008. *How Your Child Learns Best: Brain-Friendly Strategies You Can Use to Ignite Your Child's Learning and Increase School Success.* Naperville, IL: Sourcebooks, Inc.

Wyoming School Health and Physical Education. 2001. "Standards, Assessment, and Beyond." Retrieved May 25, 2006 from http://www.uwyo.edu/wyhpenet.

Contents of the Digital Resource CD

Pages	Lesson	Filename
29–34	Connecting with Affixes and Roots	affixesandroots.pdf
35–42; 34	Connecting with the Bill of Rights	billofrights.pdf
43–46; 34	Connecting with Volume	connectingwithvolume.pdf
47–53	Noticing Nouns	noticingnouns.pdf
54–59	Geography Gurus	geographygurus.pdf
60–62	Expression Einsteins	expressioneinsteins.pdf
63–65	Overtly Observant	overtlyobservant.pdf
66–69	Evaluating Revisions	evaluatingrevisions.pdf
70–72; 69	Comparing 2-D Shapes	comparing2dshapes.pdf
73–75; 69	Resource Comparison	resourcecomparison.pdf
76–93	Transitional Phrases	transitionalphrases.pdf
94–95	Historical Contributions	historicalcontributions.pdf
96–105	Light Examples	lightexamples.pdf
106–108	Support That Statement	supportthatstatement.pdf
109–115	Origin of Our Rights	originofourrights.pdf
116–118	Evidence to Support Point of View	pointofview.pdf
119–126	Parts of Speech	partsofspeech.pdf
127–128	Amending the Constitution	amendingtheconstitution.pdf
129–130	That's the Order	thatstheorder.pdf
131–136	Convert It	convertit.pdf
137–139	Food Chain Accordion	foodchain.pdf
140–141	Shades of Meaning Accordion	shadesofmeaning.pdf
142–143	Replacing with Equivalent Fractions	equivalentfractions.pdf
144–145	Let's Study Water Forms	waterforms.pdf
146–147	Let's Study Figurative Language	figurativelanguage.pdf

Pages	Additional Resource	Filename
12–19	Strategy Overviews	strategyoverviews.pdf
25–27	Standards Chart	standards.pdf

Notes

Notes

#51182—*Brain-Powered Lessons to Engage All Learners*